WILLIAM A. STRANG.

AUTOMOBILE INSURANCE RATE REGULATION
The Public Control of Price Competition

Automobile Insurance Rate Regulation

The Public Control of Price Competition

By

Frederick G. Crane

Assistant Professor of Business Administration
Drake University

BUREAU OF BUSINESS RESEARCH MONOGRAPH NUMBER 105

Published By

BUREAU OF BUSINESS RESEARCH
COLLEGE OF COMMERCE AND ADMINISTRATION
THE OHIO STATE UNIVERSITY
COLUMBUS, OHIO

In Cooperation With

THE GRIFFITH FOUNDATION

COLLEGE OF COMMERCE AND ADMINISTRATION
JAMES R. McCOY, *Dean*

BUREAU OF BUSINESS RESEARCH STAFF
VIVA BOOTHE, *Director*
JAMES C. YOCUM, *Associate Director (Marketing)*
MIKHAIL V. CONDOIDE, *Economics*   RALPH M. STOGDILL, *Personnel*
PAUL G. CRAIG, *Economics*   OMAR GOODE, *Tabulations*

RESEARCH ASSISTANTS

RONALD BRADY   JAMES NEUHART
JEANETTE FILSINGER   DAVID POTTER
MARY MARTIN   RODERICK PURCELL
MARTHA STRATTON

FOREWORD

This study is concerned with the systematic presentation and analysis of the many aspects of public control of price competition in the automobile insurance business through automobile insurance rate regulation. Among the many facets of the subject considered are: the historical development and structure of the automobile insurance market; the types of insurers; the instruments of control and their development; and the issues and problems involved in control.

The Bureau of Business Research wishes to acknowledge the substantial contribution toward publication of the study made to the Bureau by The Charles W. Griffith Memorial Foundation for Insurance Education.

Viva Boothe, Director

PREFACE

Few subjects discussed in the property-casualty insurance business in recent years have created more interest than that of rate regulation. This is as it should be, as few subjects will be of greater importance to the business in the years ahead.

In spite of all that has been said and written about rate regulation, it has been extremely difficult to form objective judgments of the issues involved. This has been true partly because so much of the discussion has been from the viewpoint of a particular vested interest: stock insurer, mutual insurer, agency system, direct-writing system, bureau, or independent company. In addition, much of the consideration has focused upon certain isolated aspects of rate regulation without viewing them in the perspective of the over-all problem and its historical development. Thus, for example, debate raged yesterday over the right of partial subscribership; today, it concerns prior approval; tomorrow some other specific issue will be the center of attention.

To the discussion which has preceded it, this study adds little which is new. The intention, instead, is to identify the various reasons for rate regulation, to draw together much of what has been said and done about the subject, and to present these things in a manner which will provide a basis for analysis of the fundamental issues involved. It is hoped that this will contribute to the solution of specific regulatory issues as they arise in the future.

Those who disagree with the conclusions which I have reached, therefore, have grounds for regarding them as being of less importance than the analysis which precedes them. It seems proper to add, however, that I feel my judgments to be colored by a minimum of prejudice. Over periods totalling in excess of five years, I have been closely associated with two companies which hold opposing viewpoints on many regulatory issues, one being a large, very old, stock, American agency system, bureau company; the other, a relatively younger and smaller mutual, direct writing, independent company. In addition, I have devoted an equal period of time to the study of economics and insurance in various ivory towers far removed from the tumult and shouting.

While they are in no way responsible for any shortcomings of this study, I would like to express my indebtedness to a number of people who knowingly or unknowingly have contributed to its fulfillment. Valuable counsel was provided by my dissertation committee, consisting of Professors Edison L. Bowers, Arthur D. Lynn, Jr., and David L. Bickelhaupt. Assistance was also received from Mr. Paul R. Gingher, Mr. Knox Stewart, Mr. Arthur I. Vorys, and Dr. William H. Wandel, each of whom read the manuscript. A special word of gratitude is in order for Professor Bowers and Professor John S. Bickley, who were responsible for rekindling my interest in insurance at a critical point in my career several years ago. Also, I would like to acknowledge the contributions of those many observers and practitioners of insurance whose comments have formed an esssential part of the development of rate regulation and of this study.

Finally, I am doubly indebted to the Charles W. Griffith Memorial Foundation for Insurance Education. First, the Foundation's award of the Murray D. Lincoln Fellowship for the academic year 1960–1961 made the research financially feasible. Second, the publication of the study was partially underwritten by the Griffith Foundation through a substantial contribution toward the cost of printing to the Bureau of Business Research.

F. G. CRANE

TABLE OF CONTENTS

TABLE OF CONTENTS (Continued)

TABLE OF CONTENTS (Continued)

LIST OF TABLES

FOOT NOTES
?

CHAPTER I

INTRODUCTION

STATEMENT OF THE PROBLEM

[In each of the fifty states, laws have been adopted[1] and executive departments established for the purpose of regulating the business of insurance. Among the many aspects of this regulation is control of the rates charged for numerous forms of insurance. The casualty and surety rate regulatory laws in force in the great majority of the states include the following statement of purpose: '

[The purpose of this Act is to promote the public welfare by regulating insurance rates to the end that they shall not be excessive, inadequate or unfairly discriminatory, and to authorize and regulate cooperative action among insurers in rate making and in other matters within the scope of this Act. Nothing in this Act is intended (1) to prohibit or discourage reasonable competition, or (2) to prohibit or encourage except to the extent necessary to accomplish the aforementioned purpose, uniformity in insurance rates, rating systems, rating plans or practices.[2]]

[In requiring that rates be neither excessive nor inadequate, while at the same time authorizing competition, the laws imply that there is a zone of reasonableness above which rates are too high and below which they are too low.]With the exception of a few states, however, the statutes contain no definition of "excessive" or "inadequate." [It is left to the insurance commissioner to determine the location and amplitude of the zone within which rate levels are proper.]The result has been that even though the laws in the various states are substantially the same in text, their interpretation has varied "according to the views and backgrounds of the insurance

[1] For citations see Donovan, James B., "Rate Regulation Revisited," *Insurance and Government* (University of Wisconsin Insurance Series, Vol. II, No. 4; Madison, Wisconsin: Fund for Insurance Education and Research, 1960), pp. 7–9.

[2] All Industry Bill: Casualty and Surety Rate Regulatory bill. Quoted in U. S., Congress, Senate, Subcommittee on Antitrust and Monopoly of the Committee on the Judiciary. *Hearings on the Insurance Industry*, 85th Congress and 86th Congress, 1958, 1959, 1960, pp. 5007–5021. These Hearings will hereafter be cited as "Insurance Hearings."

commissioner and according to the traditions or precedents of his office."[3]

[The determination of insurance rates involves the application of actuarial techniques to masses of statistical data. It might therefore seem that rate making would be a scientifically exact process and that the responsibility of the rate regulator would be limited to checking the mathematical accuracy of the computation.] However, actuaries themselves caution that it is not this simple.

> It is the casualty actuary's task in interpreting the statistical and other pertinent evidence to develop rates proper for the period of their application, which fall within a "zone of reasonableness" that will stand the test of probing criticism in satisfying jointly the criteria that a rate shall not be excessive, inadequate or unfairly discriminatory. These criteria, even considered jointly, are comparatively subjective in character, not being determinable in unassailably objective terms.[4]

> In the final analysis it must be re-emphasized that the determination of rates is not an automatic process but that judgment enters that determination at every step of the way, whether the rates be established on the basis of a formula or whether they be established as a direct result of judgment considerations.[5]

Just as rate making requires the use of judgment by the actuary, so must the supervision of rates depend upon the exercise of judgment by the regulator. In each instance, public welfare demands that the judgment be honest and intelligent. The integrity of insurance regulators as a whole has never been seriously challenged; it is not an issue. But the ability of any individual to reach proper decisions in a matter so complex and about which so little is known as insurance rate regulation has been questioned increasingly in recent years.[It is one thing to say that rates shall not be excessive, inadequate, or unfairly discriminatory, it has been said, and "another thing to apply these standards with a clear and uniform idea in mind as to what they mean for all insurers and insureds."[6]]

[3] National Association of Insurance Commissioners, "Report of Insurance All-Industry Committee Respecting the Matter of Interstate Cooperation or Compacts," *Proceedings,* 1951, p. 161.

[4] Carlson, Thomas O., "Rate Regulation and the Casualty Actuary," *Proceedings of the Casualty Actuarial Society,* Vol. XXXVIII, Part i, No. 69 (May 1951), p. 16.

[5] *Ibid.,* p. 41. The role of judgment in casualty rate making is further explained in Leslie, William, "Casualty Problems from the Public Viewpoint," *Proceedings of the Casualty Actuarial Society,* Vol. XI, No. 23 (1924), pp. 2–8.

[6] Cowee, John W., and Center, Charles C., *Federal Regulation of Insurance* (Wisconsin Commerce Reports, Vol. II, No. 3; Madison, Wisconsin: University of Wisconsin, School of Commerce, Bureau of Business Research and Service, 1949), p. 56.

The rate laws have been interpreted in various ways at various times in various states. Arthur I. Vorys, former Superintendent of Insurance of Ohio, has said:

[I defy any casualty actuary . . . to predict with certainty what any given commissioner will do with any given rate filing made pursuant to our rating laws. The lack of definite standards against which a rate may be approved or disapproved is or should be of real concern not only to every commissioner, but, even more so, to any executive trying to run a reasonably successful insurance company.[7]]

One of the relatively few serious students of the subject has stated that:

[Rate regulation is in sad shape in a lot of ways in fire and casualty insurance. It is not necessarily the fault of the people who are doing the regulating. It is because of lack of fundamental knowledge.[8]]

[An illustration will help to explain the problem. An insurance department receives rate filings from insurance companies A and B. The filings are for a kind of insurance provided statewide under idential policy forms by the two companies. Both filings include actuarial calculations based upon the particular company's loss and expense data for the previous three years. They involve identical systems of data collection and classification. The actuaries of both companies use the same technique in computing the final rate. But while the data indicate that Company A needs to charge a $70 rate in order to realize a 2.5 per cent profit margin, Company B anticipates the same profit through use of a $50 rate. The dissimilarity may be due to differences in company losses, expenses or other factors.

The Commissioner is faced with a number of problems. Should either or both rates be approved? Is $70 excessive? Is $50 inadequate? Is it not possible that $70 is inadequate and $50 excessive for these particular companies? If a number of other companies are also requesting a $70 rate, are they attempting to exploit the policy-buying public from a position of monopolistic power? Will the $50 rate permit Company B to achieve a monopolistic position? Should the Commissioner insist that there can be but one proper rate, perhaps $60?]

[7] Vorys, Arthur I., "The Responsibilities of the Insurance Commissioner," *Papers and Proceedings* (Indianapolis: National Association of Mutual Insurance Companies, 1958), p. 75.
[8] Testimony of Hedges, Robert A., *Insurance Hearings,* p. 1105.

⌐ The section of the rate law previously quoted authorizes both competition and uniformity in rates. The Commissioner accordingly might consider the problem presented by the two filings to be the achievement of a reasonable balance between price competition and price uniformity. That is, should he permit, limit, or prohibit the degree of price competition between companies A and B which would result from the two filings?

The latter statement of the problem, emphasizing the control of price competition, is the principal orientation of this study. The purpose of the study is to analyze this problem, consider the alternative answers which have been proposed, and suggest an approach to its solution. ⌐

NATURE OF THE STUDY

Insurance regulation is an enormously complex subject. One Insurance Commissioner has said: "The business of insurance and the system of its regulation by the states are so vast that no mind has ever been or will be capable of fully encompassing them."[9] The responsibilities of the state insurance departments extend from the organization of insurers to their liquidation. Supervision includes such diverse matters as the licensing of agents, approval of policy forms, regulation of investments, requirement of reserves, conduct of examinations, and investigation of public complaints. It has been estimated that a tenth of all state legislation deals either directly or indirectly with insurance.[10]

⌐Rate regulatory statutes alone include:
1. Laws designed to prevent inadequate rates.
2. Laws designed to prevent excessive rates.
3. Laws designed to prevent unfair rate discrimination.
4. Laws regulating rate making organizations.
5. Laws requiring the filing of rates, rules and rating plans.

Closely related statutes include:
6. Laws designed to prevent unfair price competition.
7. Laws relating to policy forms.
8. Laws regulating dividend payments.
9. Laws relating to agents and acquisition costs.
10. Laws governing company reserves.[11] ⌐

[9] Testimony of F. Britton McConnel, Insurance Commissioner of California, *Insurance Hearings*, p. 1861.

[10] Kulp, C. A., *Casualty Insurance* (3d ed.; New York: Ronald Press, 1956), p. 557.

[11] Hobbs, Clarence W., "State Regulation of Insurance Rates," *Proceedings of the Casualty Actuarial Society*, Vol. XXVIII, No. 58 (May 1942), p. 344.

This study concentrates upon rate regulation and, more specifically, upon the standards of rate adequacy and excessiveness. The third rate standard, which prohibits unfair discrimination in rates, is considered only as it relates to the general level of rates and the "zone of reasonableness."[12]

Within the subject of rate regulation, the investigation is further confined to the field of automobile insurance.[13] Automobile insurance was selected because of its importance and because its regulation has been the subject of much controversy in recent years. It is believed however, that the analysis and findings are relevant to the regulation of all lines of insurance.

A further limitation imposed upon the study is the assumption that rate regulation will continue to be a responsibility of the state governments. The relative merits of state and federal control are not considered.[14]

In addition, it is assumed that a privately owned and operated insurance industry is in the public interest, with governmental control limited to the amount of regulation necessary for proper public protection.

One of the things which makes insurance regulation, and indeed, the whole field of insurance, a fascinating subject is the fact that there are so many possible approaches to it. One can concentrate upon the problems of law, emphasizing legal precedents, interpretations, and remedies; many have done so. Or accounting, actuarial or financial matters may be stressed. The intention here is not to focus upon any of these particular aspects, and purposely to avoid extensive treatment of accounting, actuarial, financial, or legal details. Instead, the orientation is upon the basic economic issues involved in achieving the proper degree of public control over price

[12] The regulation of discriminatory pricing in property and casualty insurance has chiefly concerned such personal discrimination as rebating and misclassification, and such group discrimination as rate variations not proportional to cost differences among classifications of insureds. See Williams, C. Arthur, *Price Discrimination in Property and Liability Insurance* (University of Minnesota Studies in Economics and Business, No. 19; Minneapolis: University of Minnesota Press, 1959).

[13] All automobile insurance coverages, including bodily injury liability, property damage liability, medical payments, collision, comprehensive, fire, theft and combined additional coverages.

[14] For viewpoints opposing and favoring federal regulation see Statement of National Association of Insurance Commissioners, *Insurance Hearings*, pp. 4837–79, and Otto, Ingolf H. B., "Regulation of Insurance in the United States by the Federal Government" (unpublished Ph.D. dissertation, George Washington University, 1959).

competition in automobile insurance; it is, in effect, an economic approach.

It has been charged that insurance supervision is based upon assumptions about the economic environment and structure of the industry which, although valid when the regulatory statutes were originally framed fifty years ago, are no longer appropriate.[15] This study therefore begins with a survey of the automobile insurance market, concentrating upon price competition. The market survey provides the general context within which the problems of regulation are later considered and aids in reaching a judgment as to whether the current economic and competitive atmosphere has made past theories of rate regulation obsolete.

Current issues are then given historical perspective by tracing the development of public control in this field. The methods and purposes of current rate regulation are outlined.

A section is then devoted to the issue of price competition and diversity versus cooperative pricing and uniformity. The cases both for and against the restriction of price competition are developed. The orientation of this approach differs basically from much of the previous discussion of insurance rate regulation. Most of the public debate on the matter has concentrated specifically upon the rate standards and has concerned the nature of excessive or inadequate rates. Only in part or by implication has it involved what the author sees as the basic issue: the control of price competition.

In this context, administration of the excessiveness and inadequacy standards is then considered. Here the issues become: Can price competition in automobile insurance furnish reasonable protection against excessive rates? Is price competition likely to force rates down to inadequate levels? What degree of restraint upon competition is required? Which methods of control are preferable?

These issues are of more than academic interest. The Supreme Court has noted that "perhaps no modern commercial enterprise directly affects so many persons in all walks of life as does the insurance business. Insurance touches the home, the family, and the occupation or the business of almost every person in the United

[15] McHugh, Donald P., "The Role of Competition in Insurance Rate Making," *Journal of the Bar Association of the District of Columbia,* Vol. XXVI (May, 1959), p. 182.

States."[16] The total premium volume of the U. S. property and casualty insurance business in 1960 approached $15 billion.[17]

Widespread concern over these matters has been evidenced by the extensive investigation conducted during 1958, 1959, and 1960 by the Antitrust and Monopoly Subcommittee of the U.S. Senate. A special committee of the National Association of Insurance Commissioners has also conducted hearings. In addition, there has been an outpouring of articles and addresses on the subject.

[The significance of the problem is further indicated by proposals for amendment of the state rating laws. Alternative bills are being urged by several insurer associations. It appears likely that a number of state legislatures will reappraise their insurance regulatory statutes within the next few years.

This seems an appropriate time "to give the rating laws a long hard look to determine what they do and what they do not do; to determine what basic public policy they serve and how it may be served uniformly, wisely, and effectively."[18]]

[16] *United States* v. *South-Eastern Underwriters Association,* 322 U. S. 540 (1944).

[17] *Best's Fire and Casualty Aggregates and Averages* (New York: Alfred M. Best Co., 1961), p. 1.

[18] Vorys, Arthur I., *loc. cit.,* p. 76.

CHAPTER II

THE AUTOMOBILE INSURANCE MARKET

HISTORICAL DEVELOPMENT

Automobile insurance in the United States was first written in 1898 when the Travelers Insurance Company wrote a liability policy covering a Buffalo, New York, physician.[1] The coverage was provided by modifying the policy form commonly used at the time for insuring the operation of horse-drawn vehicles.

Some companies were at first highly reluctant to insure the newly-developed horseless carriages. The president of a large casualty company is reported as saying around 1900:

> We would not write liability insurance on a railroad train, running on steel rails, through protected property, and under the control of a skilled engineer who had spent years learning how to do it. Then wouldn't we be nitwits to write such insurance covering an automobile, traveling at breakneck speed over highways and byways, in open spaces, through the center of villages and cities, over railroad crossings, and driven by anybody who had enough money to buy one of the contraptions whether or not he had enough brains properly to operate it.[2]

Within a few years, however, as automobile registrations climbed rapidly,[3] many companies were competing strongly for the new source of premium income. But premium volume did not rise as spectacularly as automobile usage. In 1927, Patterson alluded to automobile coverage as being one of the "minor forms of insurance."[4] Premium volume did not reach the half-billion dollar mark until 1937[5] when almost 30 million vehicles were registered. It was after

[1] Kahn, Harry A., "Liability Insurance Rates: Automobile Liability," *Examination of Insurance Companies*, Vol. V (New York: New York State Insurance Department, 1955), p. 69.

[2] Caverly, Raymond N., "The Background of the Casualty and Bonding Business in the United States," *Insurance Counsel Journal*, Vol. VI, No. 4 (October 1939), p. 64.

[3] Table 1.

[4] Patterson, Edwin W., *The Insurance Commissioner in the United States* (Cambridge: Harvard University Press, 1927), p. 270.

[5] Table 2.

TABLE 1—Motor Vehicle Registrations, United States, Annually, 1895-1960

Year	Registrations	Year	Registrations
1895	4	1928	24,511,683
1896	16	1929	26,502,508
1897	90	1930	26,531,999
1898	800	1931	25,862,038
1899	3,200	1932	24,132,609
1900	8,000	1933	23,876,707
1901	14,800	1934	24,954,004
1902	23,000	1935	26,229,743
1903	32,920	1936	28,172,318
1904	55,290	1937	29,706,158
1905	78,800	1938	29,442,705
1906	108,100	1939	30,615,087
1907	143,200	1940	32,035,424
1908	198,400	1941	34,472,145
1909	312,000	1942	32,578,925
1910	468,500	1943	30,499,608
1911	639,500	1944	30,086,189
1912	944,000	1945	30,638,429
1913	1,258,060	1946	33,945,817
1914	1,763,018	1947	37,360,463
1915	2,490,932	1948	40,556,469
1916	3,617,937	1949	44,139,951
1917	5,118,525	1950	49,195,212
1918	6,160,448	1951	51,948,806
1919	7,576,888	1952	53,301,329
1920	9,239,161	1953	56,254,506
1921	10,493,666	1954	58,542,937
1922	12,273,599	1955	62,727,173
1923	15,102,105	1956	65,182,560
1924	17,612,940	1957	67,158,771
1925	19,940,724	1958	68,328,346
1926	22,052,559	1959	71,526,158
1927	23,139,559	1960	73,897,000[a]

[a] 1960 figure estimated by Automobile Manufacturers Association.

Source: *Automobile Facts and Figures* (Detroit: Automobile Manufacturers Association, 1961 edition), p. 18.

Note: 1895–1949 figures are for privately owned vehicles only. 1950–1960 figures include publicly owned vehicles other than military vehicles.

World War II that premiums shot upward. They totaled $2 billion in 1946, motor vehicle registrations having risen only to about 34 million. By 1960, 73 million vehicles were on the road and insurance premiums approached $6 billion.[6] In that year automobile premiums were greater than the entire volume of the property-casualty insur-

[6] *Ibid.*

TABLE 2—Automobile Insurance Premiums Written by Stock and Mutual Companies, by Line of Coverage, Annually, 1930-1960

Year	Bodily Injury Liability	Property Damage Liability	Physical Damage	Total
		Thousands of Dollars		
1930	$ 214,083	$ 73,812	$ 127,024	$ 414,919
1931	215,887	70,164	113,577	399,628
1932	191,245	58,743	90,000	339,988
1933	193,673	59,489	78,302	331,464
1934	203,967	61,168	93,489	358,624
1935	225,445	65,210	118,471	409,126
1936	252,156	70,898	175,619	498,673
1937	277,246	78,995	212,240	568,481
1938	277,516	78,598	179,070	535,184
1939	271,980	78,871	225,181	576,032
1940	288,471	84,080	278,725	651,276
1941	327,520	97,724	326,360	751,604
1942	321,230	102,884	191,883	615,997
1943	266,632	102,365	184,448	553,445
1944	299,957	112,283	202,566	614,806
1945	343,827	127,460	251,736	723,023
1946	478,328	185,493	410,814	1,074,635
1947	620,377	276,641	632,597	1,529,615
1948	727,993	350,709	783,869	1,862,571
1949	801,973	401,213	996,486	2,199,672
1950	886,453	451,246	1,118,723	2,456,422
1951	1,045,018	527,814	1,265,226	2,838,058
1952	1,276,470	641,432	1,512,457	3,430,359
1953	1,480,749	776,693	1,653,303	3,910,745
1954	1,556,653	809,684	1,573,506	3,939,843
1955	1,655,438	839,577	1,727,711	4,222,726
1956	1,814,019	870,262	1,613,295	4,297,576
1957	2,070,801	932,484	1,748,994	4,752,279
1958	2,297,555	1,019,167	1,773,831	5,090,553
1959	2,563,913	1,117,797	1,995,196	5,636,906
1960	2,725,035	1,157,882	1,993,930	5,876,847

Source: *Best's Fire and Casualty Aggregates and Averages* (New York: Alfred M. Best Co., 1940, 1950, 1960, 1961 editions).

ance business in 1948. They now constitute about 40 per cent of the business handled by property-casualty companies.

Roughly three out of every four American families now own an automobile[7] and many families own two or more automobiles. With

[7] *Statistical Abstract of the United States* (Washington: U. S. Department of Commerce, 1960), p. 563.

motor vehicle accidents continuing at high rates,[8] automobile insurance is regarded as an essential item in the budget of most families.[9] The price of automobile insurance, more than ever before, has become a matter of both private and public concern.

STRUCTURE OF THE MARKET[10]

Product Attributes

Legal Contract—The product of an automobile insurance company, the policy, is a legal document constituting an obligation to perform certain services if and when the insured-against contingencies occur. Specific coverages available under the policy include protection against legal liability claims, involving either bodily injury or property damage, arising out of the ownership, maintenance or use of the car. Premiums for the liability coverages constituted approximately two-thirds of the total automobile premium in 1960.[11] The other major group of coverages, accounting for one-third of the premiums, are the physical damage coverages. These reimburse the policyholder for collision and other damage to the insured automobile.

Complexity—One of the most significant attributes of the automobile policy from the regulatory viewpoint is its complexity. Once called a "masterpiece of obfuscation,"[12] it is long, involved, and full of legal and technical phraseology incomprehensible to the typical insurance buyer. Furthermore, determination of the true worth of an insurance purchase would involve an evaluation of the ability and willingness of the particular company and agent to provide the

---

[8] In the 10-year period 1950–1959 there were an estimated 100,000,000 accidents in which 376,000 people were killed and 13,500,000 suffered disabling injuries. *Accident Facts* (Chicago: National Safety Council, 1960), p. 41.

[9] It is compulsory in Massachusetts, New York, and North Carolina.

[10] The automobile insurance market will be considered under two main headings: structure and conduct. Structure is taken here to refer to the characteristics which constitute a market's patterns, status, or composition. Conduct relates to the actions, dealings, or tactics of the companies. A third aspect of the market, performance, representing the realization of normatively significant economic results will be considered in Chapter V. This division is from Sosnick, Stephen H., "A Critique of Workable Competition," *Quarterly Journal of Economics,* Vol. LXXII (August, 1958), pp. 386–423.

[11] About 46 per cent from bodily injury (and medical payments) and 19 per cent from property damage.

[12] "The Underwriters," *Fortune,* Vol. XLII (July 1950), p. 77.

promised services if a claim should arise. The inequality of knowledge and bargaining power between buyer and seller provides one of the justifications for public supervision of insurance.

Demand—"No one . . . has seriously undertaken to trace the source of insurance markets and to describe the relation of insurance premiums to the real world."[13] We do know, of course, that the demand for automobile insurance is closely related to the demand for automobiles. The two are complementary goods; the acquisition of one raises the utility of the other.[14]

It appears likely that the demand for automobile insurance (particularly the liability coverages) is highly inelastic. Its cost is small relative to the total cost of automobile transportation, and there is no satisfactory substitute commodity. In some instances, purchase of insurance is mandatory. This is true not only in the states having compulsory insurance laws. In many other instances, state financial responsibility laws require liability insurance of some persons as a result of accidents or convictions; for other drivers these laws provide added inducement to purchase the coverage. In addition, physical damage coverage is commonly required by lending institutions financing the purchase of automobiles.

These elements of compulsion, together with the desire to eliminate the economic insecurity involved in automobile ownership, support the belief that the consumers of automobile insurance are relatively unresponsive to industry-wide price changes. This is further borne out by the fact that the percentage of disposable personal income devoted to the purchase of automobile insurance has risen since World War II[15] in spite of the substantial increases that have occurred in the level of rates.

In addition, estimates of the percentage of vehicles insured indicate a steady rise during the period of rate increases. Approximately one-third of all registered automobiles were covered in 1930, slightly

[13] Rennie, Robert A., "One Out of Three," *Best's Insurance News*, October, 1959, p. 82. All citations of this publication are of the Fire and Casualty Edition.

[14] Norris, Ruby Turner, *The Theory of Consumer's Demand* (rev. ed.; New Haven: Yale University Press, 1952), p. 12. "Alternatively we may frame a definition in terms of demand price as follows: goods are complementary if a consumer would pay more for them in combination than he would pay for the goods if they were to be utilized separately." *Ibid.*, p. 130.

[15] Table 3.

TABLE 3—Disposable Personal Income and Automobile Insurance Premiums
Written, Annually, 1930-1960

Year	Disposable Personal Income	Automobile Insurance Premiums	Premiums as Percentage of Income
	Billions of Dollars		%
1930	$ 74.4	$ .415	0.56
1931	63.8	.400	0.63
1932	48.7	.340	0.70
1933	45.7	.331	0.72
1934	52.0	.359	0.69
1935	58.3	.409	0.70
1936	66.2	.499	0.75
1937	71.0	.468	0.80
1938	65.7	.535	0.81
1939	70.4	.576	0.82
1940	76.1	.651	0.86
1941	93.0	.752	0.81
1942	117.5	.616	0.52
1943	133.5	.553	0.41
1944	146.8	.615	0.42
1945	150.4	.723	0.48
1946	160.6	1.075	0.67
1947	170.1	1.530	0.90
1948	189.3	1.863	0.98
1949	189.7	2.200	1.16
1950	207.7	2.456	1.18
1951	227.5	2.838	1.25
1952	238.7	3.430	1.44
1953	252.5	3.911	1.55
1954	256.9	3.940	1.53
1955	274.4	4.223	1.54
1956	292.9	4.298	1.47
1957	308.8	4.752	1.54
1958	317.9	5.091	1.60
1959	337.3	5.637	1.67
1960	354.2	5.877	1.66

Source: *Economic Report of the President* (Washington: U. S. Government Printing
Office, 1961), p. 143 and Table 2.

under one-half in 1945, and about two-thirds in 1946.[16] Today about
85 per cent are insured for liability with a smaller proportion carrying the physical damage coverages.[17] This is further evidence of inelastic demand conditions.

[16] Deyo, James E., "The American Agency System," *Best's Insurance News*, September
1959, p. 59.
[17] *Ibid*. A 1957 study found 84 per cent of the automobiles insured for liability, 57
per cent for collision, and 70 per cent for comprehensive. *The National Underwriter*, August
21, 1959, p. 8.

The principal exception to the foregoing discussion is probably the demand for physical damage coverage on older cars. This coverage is not required by law, and a smaller proportion of such cars is being financed at any given time. Decisions as to whether or not to insure such vehicles against damage are undoubtedly strongly influenced by price considerations. With this exception, it appears that the demand for automobile insurance is highly inelastic.

It may be concluded that the most important determinants of the long-run demand for automobile insurance are the number of vehicles in use, legal requirements for coverage, and requirements of financing institutions. Any extensive analysis of the secular trend of this demand might include consideration of such additional variables as current and prospective income, population, automobile prices, financing terms, quality and quantity of public transportation, and even the political atmosphere in state legislatures. A factor which will be of less significance in future long-range demand will be independent decisions of previously uninsured drivers to buy insurance. In this sense the market has become quite well saturated; competition by insurers for business will have to concentrate upon new drivers and upon those already covered by rival carriers.

Cyclical variations in the demand for automobile insurance are of minor significance. This is evident in Table 3 and is consistent with what has been said about the nature of the demand conditions.

It is true, of course, that the demand for automobiles is closely related to current and expected income.[18] But in periods of declining personal income, a contraction in car purchases can occur without a significant drop in car usage. From 1929 to 1933, new car sales dropped 65 per cent, while total registrations fell only 10 per cent.[19]

As would be expected, short-run fluctuations are greater for physical damage than for liability coverages. Total physical damage premiums written by stock companies in 1933 were 46 per cent below the 1929 level. In the same period, liability premiums declined only 18 per cent.[20] Total liability premiums have risen every

---

[18] Chow, G. C., Demand for Automobiles in the United States ("Contributions to Economic Analysis" Vol. XIII; Amsterdam: North-Holland Publishing Co., 1957).

[19] *The National Underwriter,* January 29, 1960, p. 27.

[20] *Best's Fire and Casualty Aggregates and Averages* (New York: Alfred M. Best Co., 1960), p. 27.

year since World War II; physical damage volume dipped in 1954 and 1956.[21]

Detailed analysis of premium volume would reveal other fluctuations in the rate of increase. To a great extent, however, these would reflect changes in the per-car premium rates and would not alter the belief that the demand for automobile insurance is highly inelastic and little subject to cyclical variation.

Production Characteristics

Low Fixed Costs—The insurance business is characterized by extremely low fixed costs. The provision of insurance protection involves minimal amounts of plant, equipment, raw material stock, or inventory. Office space and accounting and communications equipment, of course, are essential, but the principal resources are capital funds and skilled manpower. Over four-fifths of the total expected costs of most automobile policies are variable costs. The two chief components of the rate filing illustrated in Table 4 are variable costs: production cost (predominantly agents' commissions) and losses plus allocated claim expense. Other variable costs include

TABLE 4—Provisions in Automobile Bodily Injury Liability Rates, New York, Bureau Filing of March 31, 1959

Provision	Per Cent
Expenses (excluding claim expense)	
General administration	5.37
Inspection, exposure audit, and bureau	.97
Production cost	20.00
Taxes, licenses, and fees	4.85
Subtotal	31.19
Losses and claim expense	
Unallocated loss adjustment	5.94
Losses and allocated claim expense	59.45
Subtotal	65.39
Profit and contingencies	3.42
Total	100.00

Source: *Insurance Hearings*, p. 4367.

[21] Table 2.

state premium taxes (usually 2 per cent of premium), and much of the underwriting, policy issuance and policy maintenance expense.

Entry—Barriers to the entry of new firms into the industry exist, but are often over-emphasized. Capital and surplus requirements vary from state to state. In some states they are $500,000 or more; in others, as low as $15,000. A few states still have no statutory requirements.[22] Company formation does of course involve additional financial requirements in the form of working capital and physical facilities. But the total outlay required is small when an automobile insurer is compared, for example, with an automobile manufacturer.

Access to the necessary technology is not a significant barrier to entry. Insurance techniques are not protected by patent rights, and a large supply of trained personnel exists, although there is considerable competition for it.

Access to consumer markets is a more serious impediment to the formation of new insurers. Formerly, new companies faced rules which were openly promulgated and enforced by dominant company organizations anxious to protect their markets and methods.[23] Such devices are now generally illegal. However, a new insurance enterprise still must invest considerable time, effort and talent in the struggle to gain access to the consumer market. It will find that many policyholders feel a sense of loyalty to their insurer, particularly if they have received satisfactory loss settlements, while others are wary of doing business with a new firm. One of the greatest obstacles to success in the insurance business is the great expense involved in building the large and efficient agency and sales-management force needed to secure the desired premium volume. In order to attract insureds and agents, new entrants may find it necessary to offer either premium concessions, high agency commissions, or both. That many young companies manage to overcome these difficulties, however, is evident in the record of successful new ventures.[24]

[22] U. S., Congress, Senate, Subcommittee on Antitrust and Monopoly of the Committee on the Judiciary. *The Insurance Industry: Aviation, Ocean Marine, and State Regulation,* Report No. 1834, 86th Congress, 2nd Session, 1960, p. 187. This report will hereafter be cited as "First Insurance Report."

[23] Stelzer, Irwin M., "Economic Consequences of a Successful Antitrust Prosecution," *Insurance Law Journal,* No. 373 (February, 1954), p. 89.

[24] See discussion following in this section.

Even if entry to the business were free from artificially imposed barriers, the existence of substantial economies of large-scale operation might serve to dissuade prospective entrants. From the limited evidence available, it does not appear that such economies are of decisive importance in the property-casualty insurance field.

One must be very cautious, however, in drawing conclusions about economies of scale from comparisons of company expense ratios. This is so because of the wide differences among companies with respect to such things as rate levels, agency systems, types of business underwritten, and rates of growth. "Comparisons on a basis of classes of business written may not be proper because of varying methods of operation. Likewise, comparisons on a basis of methods of operation may not be proper because of varying classes of business underwritten."[25]

One researcher, R. J. Hensley,[26] analyzed the expense data for 127 property-casualty company groups of various sizes as shown in Table 5.

TABLE 5—Total Average Expense by Size and Type of Insurance
Group, 1953

Size of Group (Thousands of Dollars)	Number of Groups			Average Expense Ratio		
	Stock	Mutual	Total	Stock	Mutual	Total
Under 5,000	15	0	15	37.7	—	37.7
5,000– 9,999	17	1	18	38.1	34.9	37.9
10,000– 24,999	31	3	34	39.6	26.8	38.5
25,000– 49,999	21	2	23	36.8	21.0	35.4
50,000– 99,999	17	3	20	37.2	18.5	34.4
100,000–249,999	12	1	13	36.0	13.6	34.3
250,000 and over	4	0	4	31.6	—	31.6

Source: Heasley, Roy J., "An Evaluation of the Performance of the Property Insurance Industry" (Unpublished Ph.D. dissertation, University of California, 1955), p. 87.

From these data, Hensley draws the following conclusions:

The 127 groups comprise most of the industry. The expense data for these groups indicate that there are economies of scale available to larger firms. . . . The tentative conclusion is that a new insurance firm may experience some difficulty in getting established because of the lower expense ratios of larger firms. However, among stock company groups significant expense

25 "Operating Expenses," Best's Insurance News, December 1959, p. 15.
26 Hensley, Roy J., "An Evaluation of the Performance of the Property Insurance Industry" (Unpublished Ph.D. dissertation, University of California, 1955).

savings do not appear until the largest groups are reached. When this fact is considered with the widespread use of uniform prices, which appear to cover the cost of nearly all firms, the importance of economies of scale as a deterrent to entry seem small. . . .

In comparison with the industrial sector of the economy, there are not any appreciable barriers to entry in property and casualty insurance.[27]

Other persons have reached different conclusions. Professor Hedges presented figures at the Senate Insurance Hearings which led him to conclude that "it is definitely true while there are inefficient large companies and efficient small companies, expense difference is definitely associated as a generalization with company size."[28] However, a rebuttal of this judgment was offered in a statement submitted by the Insurance Company of North America. The company presented data indicating that with increasing premium volume, expense ratios tend to rise up to a certain point (somewhere between one and ten million dollars of volume) and then fall for larger companies. But counterbalancing these figures, there was shown to be a tendency for loss ratios to increase with company size. The company concluded:

When the loss ratio and expense ratio are combined, it indicates that there is not a great deal of difference by size of company. There will naturally be differences based on chance alone. But the magnitude of differences between the various companies seems to indicate that size alone is not a sufficient criteria on which to judge the effectiveness of company operations.[29]

It is possible that economies of scale will be more significant in the future. Increased uses of electronic data processing and other forms of automation may improve the efficiency of large firms relative to smaller ones which cannot as effectively utilize such equipment.[30] Also, the advantage of larger firms in recruiting, developing and retaining skilled management and agency personnel may be enhanced in future years.[31]

At the present time no one knows what the optimum size of insurance companies is. There are both efficient and inefficient com-

[27] *Ibid.*, pp. 87–88.
[28] *Insurance Hearings*, p. 1089.
[29] *Ibid.*, p. 1118.
[30] Smaller firms may be able to overcome this problem to an extent through cooperative ownership and use of high-cost electronic equipment. One such venture was put into operation in 1957. *The National Underwriter*, November 14, 1957, p. 15.
[31] Rennie, Robert A., *op. cit.*, pp. 81–82.

panies of all sizes. It seems valid to say "it has not been demonstrated that economies of scale decisively affect the competitive struggle in the insurance industry."[32]

What has been said thus far about the lack of effective obstacles to entry is corroborated by the data on actual company formations. According to records kept by the American Mutual Insurance Alliance, 8,957 property-casualty insurers have been organized in the history of the United States. Some 5,678 of these have retired from business for one reason or another (many having been absorbed by other companies), leaving 3,279 in operation as of April 1, 1961.[33] During the period 1953-1957, 678 new domestic insurance companies of all kinds were licensed, and a total of 6,581 admittances were granted to foreign and alien companies by the various states.[34] In the same period, 355 insurers were totally liquidated or reinsured.[35] In the Spring of 1959 it was stated that of approximately 1,200 property-casualty companies listed in *Best's Insurance Reports,* 343 had been established since 1946.[36] In 1942 a total of 181 companies were writing automobile bodily injury liability coverage in the United States. By 1957, 645 companies were writing this coverage.[37]

It is concluded that there are few serious obstacles to entry into the automobile insurance business. While entry is not completely free, the restraints are relatively minor, particularly when compared with those encountered by public utility and oligopolistic manufacturing industries which involve huge capital investment and clear economies of scale.

Supply—The conditions under which automobile insurance is "produced" give every indication of a relatively elastic supply curve. Supply elasticity, with the quantity of insurance supplied being readily adjusted to changes in demand conditions, is consistent with

[32] McHugh, Donald P., "Rate Regulation Revisited: The Point of View of a Federal Official," *Insurance and Government* (University of Wisconsin Insurance Series, Vol. II, No. 4; Madison, Wisconsin: Fund for Insurance Education and Research, 1960), p. 99.

[33] Letter from Mr. H. F. Swanson, Assistant Manager and Secretary, American Mutual Insurance Alliance, Chicago, Ill., April 14, 1961.

[34] *First Insurance Report,* p. 214.

[35] *Ibid.,* p. 229.

[36] Gerber, Joseph F., "A Regulator Faces the Facts," *Journal of Insurance,* Vol. XXVI, No. 1 (Spring, 1959), p. 53.

[37] Testimony of Thomas C. Morrill, Vice President, State Farm Mutual Automobile Insurance Co., *Insurance Hearings,* p. 1299.

the low fixed costs and easy entry which prevail in the insurance business. The record of frequent successful entrance into the field (and frequent exit from it) is further indication of supply elasticity.

It is sometimes said that the law of supply and demand does not apply to insurance. Generally, this involves a misunderstanding of the nature of an elastic supply curve, as in the following statements:

> The law of supply and demand is not applicable to insurance . . . the supply of insurance is susceptible to enormous increase at a moment's notice, and, for practical purposes, is never short. Thus there is always competition for the acceptable available business. The demand never exceeds the supply. When competition persuades the underwriters to accept bad business at too low a price, disaster follows.[38]

> Commodities generally are produced under such conditions that the supply at any given time can be increased only at greater cost. The pressure of competition between buyers therefore tends to increase the price. . . . But there is no natural limit to the supply of insurance. . . . Since buying pressure can not exhaust the market it does not tend to higher prices.[39]

If the supply curve of insurance is visualized as rising only very slowly from left to right, with price being determined at the intersection with an almost vertical demand curve, the situation becomes more clear.

With a highly elastic supply curve a modest growth of demand will require but a very small price increase, perhaps not a sufficient increase to justify the expense of making the change, particularly if the price is regulated. Furthermore, if the increase in demand is substantial and if the capacity of the industry is easily augmented, either by the expansion of existing firms or the entry of new ones, the supply curve may shift to the right thus preventing the price rise which otherwise would occur.

Supply of automobile insurance at a given price is not unlimited. This was illustrated by the capacity problem which arose in the years immediately following World War II. During that period inflation and increased automobile usage caused the demand curve to shift to the right.[40] Even if the insurers had been able to secure ap-

---

[38] Marryott, Franklin J., "Why Regulate Insurance Rates?" *Report of Proceedings of the Section of Insurance Law* (New York: American Bar Association, 1946), p. 310.

[39] Mowbray, A. H., "Competition and Regulation of Rates for Casualty Insurance," *Proceedings of the Casualty Actuarial Society*, Vol. VIII, No. 17 (1921), pp. 7–8. Also see Hobbs, Clarence W., *op. cit.*, p. 39.

[40] Kellogg, Chester M., "The Capacity Problem," *Journal of the American Association of University Teachers of Insurance*, Vol. XVI, No. 1 (March, 1949), p. 6.

proval of rate increases as promptly as they were requested, they would have been unable to meet the increased demand readily. This is because of two regulations imposed in the interest of company solvency: (1) a requirement that unearned premium reserves be established on the basis of gross premiums without deduction for expenses, even though a large proportion of a company's operating expenses (including commissions) are incurred when policies are first written. This regulation causes heavy drains on the surplus of a rapidly expanding company; (2) rulings which limit premium income to a certain multiple of surplus funds.[41] These regulations, coupled with the shift in demand, forced many companies to increase their capital structure during the later 1940's.[42] Other things equal, the companies would have had to charge a higher price for insurance at this point in order to pay the premium necessary to lure the newly-required capital funds away from the other uses to which they could be put. This illustrates the "natural limit to the supply of insurance" at a given time and price, and the sloping nature of the supply curve.

It is true, as asserted in the first of the above quotations that there is always competition for the "acceptable available business," but only if that term is defined as the business for which the companies are permitted to charge an adequate price.[43] In a free market there would be no "unacceptable" business in this sense (except that involving an excessive catastrophe hazard); rather, the demand for such business would be met by supply at a higher price.

The economic principles of supply and demand do apply to insurance, and, as will be seen later, are pertinent to the subject of rate regulation.

Marketing Features

Role of the Agent—The agent or the broker[44] is the insurance company's principal contact with the public. This contact is of crucial importance for two reasons. First, it is the agent who brings

---

[41] Kulp, C. A., *op. cit.,* p. 594.

[42] "The Underwriters," *Fortune,* Vol XLII (July, 1950), p. 80.

[43] Insurers are unable to adjust their rates freely for specific exposures under the classification rating system which groups many presumably similar risks in the same rate class. See discussion later.

[44] Whereas agents represent insurance companies in securing and presenting proposals for coverage and sometimes in accepting risks, preparing policies and setting claims, brokers represent insureds, selecting the insurance companies with which the coverages are placed.

in the business. In one sense, there is no insurance product until the policy is sold; because of this, insurance agents are often called "producers." "Today, automobile insurance does not have to be sold. It has become a necessity which people buy. . . . What an insurance company or agency primarily has to sell, therefore, is not the coverage but a particular policy form, the philosophy of the company, or the service which the agent has to offer."[45]

Secondly, a company's agents must be relied upon, to a considerable extent, for the quality of business written. The necessity of carefully selecting the persons to whom policies are sold is a unique characteristic of insurance marketing. While company underwriters will scrutinize the applications submitted and attempt to eliminate those must likely to produce excessive losses, the agent (particularly in automobile insurance) is often best able to perform this function because of his personal contact with the applicant. Even if the agent makes no attempt to select his customers, the class of business he submits to the company will reflect the characteristics of his personal and business contacts. The company, therefore, must rely heavily upon its agents for both the quantity and quality of business written.

A survey of Ohio agents revealed that in 1958 commissions on automobile policies constituted 35.3 per cent of the average agency's income.[46] The agents thus have a vital financial interest in automobile insurance. Acting through numerous local, state and national associations the estimated 285,000 fire and casualty agents[47] speak with considerable influence with respect to any proposals which would affect their position. Their function and influence are pertinent to many issues of public policy.

Agency Systems—Automobile insurance is marketed through four different distribution systems:

1. The American agency system,
2. The exclusive agency system,
3. The direct-writing system,
4. The mail-order system.

[45] Lang, Frank, "Automobile Insurance Marketing," *Best's Insurance News*, June, 1955, p. 26.
[46] *The National Underwriter*, October 16, 1959, p. 32.
[47] *The National Underwriter*, November 20, 1959, p. 35.

The buyer of insurance is seldom aware that such differences exist. "This is due primarily to the apparent similarity of sales techniques at the consumer level that does not portray to the buyer the fundamental differences in philosophy upon which these different systems base their operations."[48] To the people in the business, however, the distinctions are of extreme importance. Each system is defended by its proponents with a zeal which sometimes seems fanatical; rival systems are denounced with equal enthusiasm.

The American agency system dominated the property-casualty field prior to World War II with such companies as Travelers, Aetna Casualty, and Hartford Accident in the fore. Since then the other methods of distribution have become increasingly important, particularly in the automobile and dwelling fire-insurance lines.

> The American agency system [companies subscribe] to the philosophy that each insured in an individual in need of personalized and special services if he is to be properly insured. It is their belief that this philosophy can be made operational only through independent local entrepreneurs especially trained in the field of insurance coverages and risk analysis who will serve the interests of the policyholder competently. Second, it is expected that these representatives also will serve the interests of the insurance carrier since they are remunerated in the form of commissions expressed as a percentage of premiums written. Furthermore, the agent is not prohibited from representing a number of insurance carriers because it is believed that to carry out his obligation to the insured it is necessary that he have a selection of insurance markets to offer.[49]

The leading exclusive agency system companies in the automobile field are State Farm Mutual, Allstate, and Nationwide Mutual. As the term indicates, the agents of these companies are prohibited from representing any other carrier. Single company representation facilitates the transfer to the company of many functions often performed under the American agency system by the agent. These functions may include policywriting, billing, collection of premiums and handling of claim matters. Through centralizing such activities in company offices where specialized personnel and the latest data processing equipment are utilized, the exclusive agency companies

---

[48] Littleton, Otis, "The Marketing Concept, Its Application to Insurance and How It Can Improve the Competitive Position of the American Agency System," *The Annals of the Society of Chartered Property and Casualty Underwriters,* Vol. XII, No. 1 (January, 1960), p. 60.

[49] *Ibid.,* p. 61.

have been able to reduce total expenses and lower the price of the insurance. Another feature of this system is that the ability of advertising to build a common identity for the company and agent in the public mind is enhanced.[50]

The direct-writing companies solicit business on a direct basis by the use of company employees. Most of the larger such companies have concentrated on commercial and industrial accounts, while a number of smaller, local direct-writing companies have sought the personal lines market.[51]

The fourth distribution system dispenses entirely with personal sales contacts, soliciting all business through the mails. Several mail-order companies have had considerable success in writing automobile coverage for a particular group of persons, such as government employees, or officers of the armed forces.

In most of the literature, the last three of these four distribution systems are lumped together and referred to as the "direct-writing system"; the companies using any of these three methods are called "direct writers." While it is hoped that more precise terminology will eventually be developed, these terms will be used here in this same manner.[52]

The main conflict has been between the American agency system companies and the direct writers, with the latter group coming on the scene after the former was apparently safely entrenched. Advocates of each system are convinced that their way of doing business is best for both the insurance business and the public; each feels that it is struggling for its own survival.[53]

Most of the controversy between representatives of the two systems has concerned the adequacy of agency service to insureds.

Many direct writers offer lower rates, which they attribute in part to a reduction of acquisition cost, accusing the independent [American agency system] agents of receiving excessive compensation for limited service.

[50] Morrill, Thomas C., "Marketing Revolution," Best's Insurance News, November, 1956, p. 36.
[51] Littleton, Otis, op. cit., pp. 62–63.
[52] Strictly speaking, only the mail-order system is "direct writing," with no salesman as an intermediary between company and insured.
[53] "Today the giants in the [American] agency company ranks have entered the arena and are engaged in an aggressive, effective challenge to their competitors . . . Two systems are in deadly clash, a process of self extermination." Cosgrove, John N., Competition in Insurance Marketing (Cincinnati: National Underwriter Co., 1960), p. 185.

The response of the independent agents is that they serve the policyholders better, as the direct writer is an employee controlled by his company.[54]

Other issues have included the claim settlement and underwriting practices employed by the opposing forces, with the air being filled with charges and counter-charges of stinginess and lack of public responsibility.

In the midst of the hostilities it is reported that the adversaries are adopting the most successful tactics of each other. Some American agency system forces are using or planning to use continuous policy forms and direct company billing. The large direct writers are decentralizing their administrative machinery, adopting the plan of deployment used by their rivals.[55]

Such intensive competition has of course created problems of public policy. Supervisory authorities must prevent rivalry among sellers from endangering the interests of the general public. This necessity may require certain limitations upon the freedom of insurers to compete.

Company Differences

Company Types—The American property-casualty insurance business is dominated by stock companies. Out of 1,166 companies listed by Best's in 1958, 730 were stock companies, 362 were mutual companies, 59 were reciprocal associations, and 15 were Lloyds organizations.[56]

In the field of automobile insurance specifically, stock companies also predominate. The top 20 company groups in earned automobile premiums for 1960 included 15 stock companies, 4 mutuals, and 1 reciprocal.[57] Table 6 indicates that the premium volume of stock companies is over twice that of mutuals.

Certain of the mutual companies, however, are very prominent individually. State Farm Mutual is the largest writer of automobile insurance with over 6 million policies in force in 1960 and earned

---

[54] Kimball, Spencer L., and Jackson, Bartlett A., "The Regulation of Insurance Marketing," *Columbia Law Review*, Vol. LXI (February, 1961), p. 160.

[55] These developments as well as the advantages and disadvantages of various aspects of the two agency systems are discussed in Bickley, John S., *Trends and Problems in the Distribution of Property-Liability Insurance* (Research Monograph No. R-91; Columbus, Bureau of Business Research, The Ohio State University, 1956), pp. 1–10 and 36–44.

[56] *Best's Insurance Reports (Fire and Casualty)* (New York: Alfred M. Best Co., 1958).

[57] *The National Underwriter*, May 26, 1961, p. 26.

TABLE 6—Automobile Insurance Premiums Written and Share of Total, Stock and Mutual Companies, Annually, 1930-1960

Year	Premiums Written		Per Cent of Total	
	Stock	Mutual	Stock	Mutual
	Thousands of Dollars		%	%
1930	$ 386,603	$ 28,416	93.2	6.8
1931	365,964	33,664	91.6	8.4
1932	299,104	40,884	88.0	12.0
1933	283,725	47,739	85.6	14.4
1934	306,008	52,616	85.3	14.7
1935	342,231	66,895	83.6	16.4
1936	420,199	78,474	84.3	15.7
1937	483,317	85,614	85.0	15.0
1938	441,808	93,376	82.6	17.4
1939	478,328	97,704	83.0	17.0
1940	540,886	110,390	83.1	16.9
1941	621,766	129,883	82.7	17.3
1942	486,281	130,716	78.9	21.1
1943	432,002	121,443	78.1	21.9
1944	471,216	135,590	77.9	22.1
1945	556,695	166,328	77.0	23.0
1946	834,803	239,832	77.7	22.3
1947	1,204,469	325,146	78.7	21.3
1948	1,471,611	390,960	79.0	21.0
1949	1,757,717	441,955	79.9	20.1
1950	1,953,256	503,166	79.5	20.5
1951	2,153,958	684,100	75.9	24.1
1952	2,607,590	822,769	76.0	24.0
1953	2,916,249	994,496	74.6	25.4
1954	2,895,170	1,044,673	73.5	26.5
1955	3,133,362	1,089,364	74.2	25.8
1956	3,113,937	1,183,639	72.5	27.5
1957	3,410,405	1,341,874	71.8	28.2
1958	3,586,040	1,504,513	70.4	29.6
1959	3,954,842	1,682,064	70.2	29.8
1960	4,096,579	1,780,267	69.7	30.3

Source: *Best's Fire and Casualty Aggregates and Averages* (New York: Alfred M. Best Co., 1940, 1950, 1960, 1961 editions).

premium of over $455 million.[58] State Farm's growth in recent years has been phenomenal; it alone accounts for 27 per cent of the increase in volume of all mutual carriers from 1949 to 1959.[59]

A number of other mutual and reciprocal carriers are leaders in

[58] *Ibid.*, p. 32.
[59] During this period, State Farm's written premium increased from $82 to $417 million while that of all mutual companies rose from $442 to $1,682 million.

certain sections of the country. These include Nationwide and Farmers Exchange, the latter a California reciprocal association.

In former years competition between stock and mutual companies aroused considerable antagonism.

> The stock-mutual conflict was once violent, though it is now much less fierce. Attacks on stock companies by mutual agents usually focused on the higher rates of the former, which allegedly went to line the pockets of stockholders. Stock agents, on the other hand, stated that mutual policies were assessable and that mutual companies were not sound financially.[60]

This controversy is now regarded as obsolete by many people and properly so, as there is little difference from the policyholder's viewpoint between well-managed stock and mutual insurers using the same distribution systems. The dispute over distribution systems does not fall along the stock versus mutual lines. Some stock companies use the American agency system and others are direct writers; the same is true of mutuals. The two largest automobile insurers, for example, are both direct writers, but one (State Farm) is a mutual and the other (Allstate) is a stock company. The ability of a company to compete depends upon the efficiency of its management, not upon its type of corporate structure.

Company Groups—A group or "fleet" of companies consists of two or more companies owned or managed by common interests. In many instances the member companies are of different types, such as casualty companies and fire companies. Other groups include a number of companies which write identical forms of insurance. An example of the latter is the America Fore Loyalty group of which 9 individual companies wrote automobile insurance in 1960.

The existence of groups of companies writing the same lines of coverage is largely a holdover from former times when the bureau stock companies dominated the business and indulged in certain restrictive practices.

> One of the restrictions adopted by the bureaus was on the number of agents any one insurance company could have in a given metropolitan center (thus effectively limiting access). Having helped establish that rule, the larger companies then acquired a number of subsidiary companies ("pups") so that they could obey the letter of the rule while securing a competitive advantage by violating its spirit.[61]

[60] Kimball, Spencer L., and Jackson, Bartlett A., *loc. cit.*
[61] Otto, Ingolf H. B., *op. cit.*, p. 31.

In 1960 there were 397 property-casualty companies in 136 groups.[62] A measure of the significance of company groups in automobile insurance is the fact that while the leading 20 individual companies earned $2.66 billion in premiums in 1960, the top 20 company groups earned $2.97 billion.[63]

Multiple-Line and Specialty Automobile Companies—Another reason for the existence of company groups is the former requirement that an automobile insurer write only certain specified lines of coverage. Until such restrictions were removed (most states had done so by the late 1940's) a casualty company, for instance, could write the automobile liability coverages but not the physical damage coverages. The opposite being true for property companies, many groups were formed to include both types of insurers so that full-coverage policies could be issued.

Today the majority of companies writing automobile insurance are multiple-line companies having the capability of writing all classes of property and casualty insurance. Some segments of the industry, however, have not chosen to exercise fully the privilege of multiple-line underwriting. Several of the leading direct writers concentrate on the most widely sold personal lines of coverage, particularly automobile and dwelling fire insurance. In contrast, a usual characteristic of American agency system companies is the writing of a greater number of lines of coverage, with considerable effort being devoted to securing large commercial and industrial accounts.

An important group of specialty companies is the physical damage insurers affiliated with sales finance companies.[64] In 1960, 65 specialty carriers (most owned by finance companies) controlled nearly one-third of the physical damage business.[65] The majority of these companies write no other line of business and confine their operations, for the most part, to insuring vehicles which are financed by their parent company. One such company (Motors Insurance Corporation), writing insurance induced by the General Motors

[62] "Stock Company Groups," *Best's Insurance News,* June 1961, p. 12.

[63] *The National Underwriter, loc. cit.*

[64] See Rokes, Willis P., "Automobile Physical Damage Affiliates of Sales Finance Companies" (unpublished Ph.D. dissertation, The Ohio State University, 1959.)

[65] *Best's Insurance Reports (Fire and Casualty)* (New York: Alfred M. Best Co., 1961). p. xi.

Acceptance Corporation, earned a total of $172 million in 1960 and was the fourth largest among all the companies in the industry.[66]

The ultimate in multiple-line operation is the provision of life insurance and property-casualty lines by a single company. Such all-line operations are prohibited in the regulations of many states. Increasing numbers of company groups, however, include both life and property-casualty companies. The number of such groups reached 143 in 1960, having increased 50 per cent in the previous three-year period.[67]

Automobile insurers fall into many categories: stock, mutual, reciprocal, Lloyds, multiple-line, specialty, group, and individual companies. The outstanding aspect of the market structure with regard to competition, however, is the division between companies using different agency systems.

Rate Making

Rating Bureaus—"No business has more incentive to cooperative effort or more to lose by failure to cooperate"[68] than the insurance business. The rates charged for insurance are based primarily upon statistical data. Their accuracy as measures of the relative probability of loss and expense, other things equal, increases with the number of insured risks represented by the data. State and federal laws recognize that in many cases only an organization receiving information from many companies can have the amount of data necessary to make reliable rates. These laws therefore permit insurance companies to form rate-making bureaus which promulgate rates based upon the statistical information supplied by the cooperating companies.[69]

Three rating bureaus are important factors in the automobile insurance market. These are the National Bureau of Casualty Underwriters, the Mutual Insurance Rating Bureau, and the National Automobile Underwriters Association. The first two make liability rates; the third handles physical damage rating.

[66] *The National Underwriter, loc. cit.*

[67] Daenzer, Bernard J., "Significant Aspects of Combined Life and Property Insurance Distribution," *The Annals of the Society of Chartered Property and Casualty Underwriters,* Vol. XII, No. 1, (January 1960), p. 88.

[68] Kulp, C. A., *op. cit.,* p. 533.

[69] This subject is discussed more fully in Chapters III and IV below.

The National Bureau of Casualty Underwriters is an outgrowth of a meeting of stock company executives in the early 1890's called for the purpose of stabilizing insurance rates.[70] In its early years, the National Bureau dominated the automobile liability field, it being the only organization which had developed the facilities for liability rate making.[71] At one point, member companies wrote 85 percent of the business.[72]

As of January 1, 1959 there were 103 member companies in the National Bureau representing 40 groups of affiliated companies. Another 204 companies subscribed to the Bureau's services.[73] Membership is open only to stock companies; subscribers include both stock and non-stock insurers. In 1959, the earned premiums of these companies in the automobile liability lines constituted about 35 per cent of the industry total.[74]

A publication of the National Bureau describes its functions in the following manner:

The Bureau (1) collects statistics from insurers, (2) develops rates and rating plans, (3) makes rate filings with state supervisory officials on behalf of its members and subscribers, (4) administers rates and rating plans, (5) develops or assists in developing policy provisions and policy forms, (6) publishes and maintains manuals of rules and rates, (7) provides a forum for discussion of matters pertaining to the business, and (8) serves as a means of communication and cooperation between regulatory authorities and insurers and with other organizations.[75]

The Mutual Insurance Rating Bureau was organized in 1929.[76] Its membership now numbers about 50 mutual insurance companies and a similar number of subscribers.[77] Whereas the National Bureau bases its rates on the experience of its members, the Mutual Bureau

[70] Kulp, C. A., *op. cit.,* p. 536.

[71] Bell, S. Alexander, "Competition," *Best's Insurance News,* October 1954, p. 29.

[72] Zoffer, H. Jerome, *The History of Automobile Liability Insurance Rating* (Pittsburgh: University of Pittsburgh Press, 1959), p. 10.

[73] Twaits, Elmer A., "Casualty and Surety Rating Bureaus," *Best's Insurance News,* April 1959, p. 29.

[74] Letter from Mr. R. L. Bornhuetter, Assistant Actuary, National Bureau of Casualty Underwirters, New York, N. Y., April 13, 1961.

[75] *National Bureau of Casualty Underwriters, A Stabilizing Influence in the Casualty Insurance Industry* (New York: National Bureau of Casualty Underwriters' Forum (1961), p. 2.

[76] Marryott, Franklin J., "Mutual Insurance Under Rate Regulation," *Law and Contemporary Problems,* Vol. XV, No. 4 (Autumn 1950), p. 559.

[77] Zoffer, H. Jerome, *op. cit.,* p. 72.

"makes its rates on the basis of combined stock and mutual experience, to the extent that combinable experience is available."[78]

The National Automobile Underwriters Association was formed in 1930, but its progenitors in physical-damage rate-making date back to 1909.[79] Stock insurers control the N.A.U.A. with its services being subscribed to by both stock and mutual companies. There are about 200 member companies and 250 subscribers.[80] The explanation for the existence of separate rating bureaus for liability and physical damage lines is found in the historical separation between the companies writing such coverages. With the advent of multiple-line insurance there appears to be no logical reason for continuing the separation; however, "traditional forms persist and the company groups which control the two national rating organizations still remain generally bound by the now wholly obsolete thinking that the automobile rating problem should be separated into two different parts, physical damage and casualty."[81]

A large and important group of companies does not use the services of any rating bureau for automobile insurance, preferring to develop their rates, risk classification systems, and policy coverages independently. The great majority of these companies belong to the National Association of Independent Insurers. The N.A.I.I. is a young organization but has been a dynamic force in the insurance business since its founding in 1945.

[The N.A.I.I. is not a rating bureau. "It does not make or file rates or forms, and it carefully avoids any action which might tend to influence its members toward uniformity in prices, products, or methods."[82] The N.A.I.I. is a national advisory organization and statistical agent which collects loss and expense statistics. The statistics are either filed with supervisory authorities on behalf of mem-

[78] Marryott, Franklin J., "Present Systems of Governmental Supervision," *Multiple-Line Insurance*, ed. Michelbacher, G. F. (New York: McGraw-Hill Book Co., 1957), p. 546.

[79] Wandel, William H., *The Control of Competition in Fire Insurance* (Lancaster, Pa.: By the author, 1935), p. 111.

[80] Magrath, J. J., "New York Insurance Rating Law and Rating Organizations," *Examination of Insurance Companies*, Vol. V. (New York: New York State Insurance Department, 1955), p. 308.

[81] Bell, S. Alexander, "Automobile Insurance Rating," *Best's Insurance News*, August 1956, p. 70.

[82] Testimony of Vestal Lemmon, General Manager, National Association of Independent Insurers, *Insurance Hearings*, p. 1201.

bers and subscribers, or are furnished to the individual companies to assist them in their own rate making.[83]

Starting with 40 member companies in 1945, the N.A.I.I. had grown to include 299 members and 71 subscribers in 1959.[84] The membership is composed of 162 stock companies, 112 mutuals, 21 reciprocals, and 4 Lloyds organizations.[85] "While the greater part of the total premiums of N.A.I.I. members is written at below-bureau levels, some . . . . companies charge rates which coincide with the bureau manual, and some others, higher than manual."[86]

Tables 7 and 8 indicate the distribution of automobile premiums among the three bureaus and the N.A.I.I. in 1957.

TABLE 7—Distribution of Automobile Bodily Injury and Property Damage Liability Written Premiums, by Rating Service, 1957

Rating Service	Bodily Injury		Property Damage	
	Premium	Per Cent	Premium	Per Cent
	Thousand Dollars	%	*Thousand Dollars*	%
N.B.C.U. Members	$ 625,190	28.7	$271,973	27.6
N.B.C.U. Subscribers	180,309	8.3	76,176	7.7
Subtotal[a]	805,500	37.0	348,150	35.3
M.I.R.B. Members	201,292	9.3	85,753	8.7
M.I.R.B. Subscribers	78,014	3.6	33,776	3.4
Subtotal	279,306	12.9	119,529	12.1
N.A.I.I. Members	624,919	28.7	292,735	29.7
N.A.I.I. Subscribers	174,880	8.0	90,516	9.2
Subtotal	799,799	36.7	383,251	38.9
All Others	291,459	13.4	135,557	13.7
Total	**$2,176,064**	**100.0**	**$986,487**	**100.0**

[a] Totals may not equal components due to rounding.
Source: *Insurance Hearings*, p. 4526.

The Structure of Rates—While requiring that the rates charged be neither excessive, inadequate nor unfairly discriminatory, the

[83] *Ibid.*
[84] *Ibid.*, p. 1195.
[85] *Ibid.*, p. 1200.
[86] *Ibid.*, p. 1201.

TABLE 8—Distribution of Automobile Physical Damage Written Premiums, by Rating Service, 1957

Rating Service	Premium	Per Cent of Total
	Thousand Dollars	%
N.A.I.I. Members and Subscribers	$ 726,519	34.8
N.A.U.A. Members and Subscribers	989,000	47.4
Other Independent Companies	370,092	17.8
Total	**$2,085,611**	**100.0**

Source: *Insurance Hearings,* p. 4528.

rate regulatory laws fail to specify the exact procedures to be used in computing the rates.[87]

Rate-making methods therefore differ among the various companies and lines of insurance. Also, the methods of computation are constantly undergoing a gradual change as unsatisfactory techniques are discarded or modified and new ones adopted.

In general, the rates established are designed to provide income sufficient for the company to (1) pay losses, (2) cover expenses of doing business, and (3) realize a margin of profit.

The specific actuarial techniques employed in rate making are not pertinent to this study.[88] However, the following description of automobile liability rate making illustrates the general principles involved:

> Automobile insurance risks are divided into rate groupings or classes according to the degree of hazard which they represent. Factors used in establishing these classes vary among the rating bureaus and independent filers, but usually give weight to the age of drivers, use of the vehicle, mileage, and, among young drivers, sex and marital status. Youthful drivers are subject to higher accident rates than are more mature operators. Moreover, since accident frequency tends to increase as road exposure increases, the automobile used for business or in driving to and from work usually falls in a higher rated class than the car used principally for pleasure driving.

> In addition to these classifications by age and use, there are rate distinctions based upon geographical locations. Thus, an automobile garaged in a metropolitan area is usually subject to a greater degree of risk than is a vehicle garaged in rural areas.

[87] Carlson, Thomas O., *op. cit.,* pp. 15–23.
[88] These are treated in detail in *Proceedings of the Casualty Actuarial Society, passim.*

The making of rates for this coverage is generally accomplished in three distinct stages which determine: (1) the prospective aggregate premiums required for the particular coverage in the state; (2) the relative share to be borne by each rating class; (3) the relative hazard of the various rating territories within the state.

The total amount of premium anticipated to be needed to conduct the line of business in the state is known as the *statewide rate level.*

The loss experience used for this purpose is that of the period considered most indicative for the purpose of prediction, since rates are made in anticipation of the experience level which will obtain during the period of their application. Usually the past experience used is that of the shortest and most recent period that will provide reasonable indications of loss costs and trends.

Since a portion of third-party liability claims are inherently subject to delay in settlement, a substantial proportion of the losses shown in recent experience are still unpaid and are simply estimates of their expected cost. To correct for the effect of over-reserving or under-reserving such pending claims, the statistical history of past outstanding losses is traced and "loss development factors" are calculated. Their purpose is to reflect the anticipated development of the current reserves for unpaid losses.

In addition to loss development factors, other trend or judgment factors may be applied.

The second step is the determination of the contribution required by each classification of risks to the total pool of premiums. Since, for this purpose, the premiums must be subdivided into groups, the amount of past statistical data required is ordinarily somewhat greater than that for rate level. This can be accomplished either by utilizing a longer experience period, or by grouping the experience of several states. Thus, a company, or group of companies, may examine the relative hazards among the classifications for its business on a country-wide rather than a state basis.

The final step is the determination of territorial relatives. Population shifts, safety and law enforcement programs, traffic density, the growth of urban areas and other factors may change the degree of hazard in individual territories and the relationship among the territories. For this reason, the relative territorial hazards as reflected in their loss experience are reviewed. In addition, surveys and judgment are used in altering the boundaries of existing rating territories and in establishing new ones.

As a result of this process, private passenger automobile rates are determined by the rates on file for each class and territory.[89]

The foregoing description pertains to class rating, which establishes a common premium for a large group or classification of risks

[89] Statement of National Association of Insurance Commissioners, *Insurance Hearings,* pp. 4932–34.

having approximately the same expected losses and expenses. Most automobile insurance is rated in this manner. In the case of large fleets of automobiles or trucks the premium is modified by other techniques to reflect the experience or characteristics of the particular risk.[90]

Table 4[91] illustrates the breakdown of provisions for losses, expenses and profit in a typical liability rate filing. The relative size of these provisions differs somewhat among various filings.[92]

Company Size and Concentration

An important aspect of market structure is the extent to which control of the market is concentrated in the hands of a few sellers. If such concentration is great, monopolistic practices are sometimes facilitated.

Several measures of concentration are used for industries other than insurance. These include physical output, employment, assets and sales. Only the latter is appropriate for the insurance business. The quantity of physical output of this business (the number of policies) would not be a significant index because the output units lack homogeneity. Data on the number of vehicles insured would be more meaningful but are not available. Neither assets nor employment would be a satisfactory index for a given line of insurance coverage—first, because most coverage is written by multiple-line companies in which it is impossible to separate the resources used for each form of coverage. Secondly, the industry employs relatively small quantities of both capital and labor, and the amount of insurance that can be handled with a given amount of these resources is rather flexible. Premium volume therefore remains as the most reliable indicator of market control in this industry.

In 1960 there were some 600 companies writing automobile insurance.[93] The 20 leading automobile insurers, by premium earned, are listed in Table 9. This Table also indicates the shifts in the ranking of the top 20 companies since 1949.

[90] These include experience, schedule and retrospective rating. See Kulp, C. A. *op. cit.*, pp. 486–532.

[91] See Table 4 earlier in the chapter.

[92] For examples see *Insurance Hearings*, pp. 4365–73.

[93] See footnote 37.

THEME STATEMENT

TABLE 9—Twenty Largest Companies, Automobile Insurance Earned Premium, 1960 and 1949

Company	1960		1949	
	Rank	Premium	Rank	Premium
		Thousand Dollars		*Thousand Dollars*
State Farm	1	$455,660	1	$86,098
Allstate	2	425,381	8	40,905
Travelers Indemnity	3	174,004	5	47,659
Motors	4	171,993	18	25,578
Nationwide Mutual	5	160,549	9	39,797
Aetna Casualty	6	159,496	12	37,936
Hartford Accident	7	141,003	3	53,923
Farmers Exchange	8	124,239	6	45,167
Liberty Mutual	9	118,743	13	36,588
U.S.F. & G.	10	117,816	7	41,091
Travelers	11	90,717	10	39,197
Lumbermens Mutual	12	79,949	4	48,437
Indemnity of North America	13	66,600	28	16,900
Government Employees	14	59,782	85	6,616
Maryland Casualty	15	59,415	20	24,070
Continental Casualty	16	55,592	29	16,541
Home	17	52,766	62	10,209
Fireman's Fund	18	52,068	51	11,914
Ohio Casualty	19	48,901	21	22,277
St. Paul Fire & Marine	20	48,506	42	13,788

Source: *The National Underwriter,* July 27, 1951, p. 4, ff; May 26, 1961, p. 25.

The 20 largest companies and company groups earned 42.6 per cent and 47.5 per cent of the premiums, respectively, in 1960. As is shown in Table 10 these percentages have increased rather steadily, but unspectacularly, since 1949.

The greatest change in market structure during recent years has been the surge of two direct writing companies, State Farm and Allstate. From 1949 to 1960 automobile insurance premiums earned by all insurers increased 153 per cent and those of the top 20 companies, 221 per cent. During the same period State Farm and Allstate premiums rose 594 per cent, the two companies accounting for almost 20 per cent of the total industry growth, and for over 40 per cent of the increases in the premiums earned by the 20 largest insurers. Table 11 shows that the percentage of the market handled by these two companies has increased from 5.1 per cent in 1949 to 14.1 per cent 12 years later.

TABLE 10—Automobile Insurance Earned Premium, Twenty Largest
Companies and Twenty Largest Company Groups, Anually, 1949-1960

Year	Earned Premium			Per Cent of Total	
	Twenty Companies	Twenty Groups	All Companies	Twenty Companies	Twenty Groups
	Thousand Dollars			%	%
1949	$ 828,563	$1,096,360	$2,468,561	33.6	44.4
1950	863,022	1,146,296	2,547,242	33.9	45.0
1951	1,000,932	1,245,864	2,882,924	34.7	43.2
1952	1,178,100	1,419,676	3,333,799	35.3	42.6
1953	1,444,585	1,723,867	3,914,244	36.9	44.0
1954	1,572,365	1,903,871	4,181,339	37.6	45.5
1955	1.652,415	1,980,152	4,381,859	37.7	45.2
1956	1,782,571	2,091,627	4,580,585	38.9	45.7
1957	1,924,744	2,308,216	4,906,820	39.2	47.0
1958	2,176,363	2,559,318	5,308,959	41.0	48.2
1959	2,428,066	2,820,844	5,818,837	41.7	48.5
1960	2,663,181	2,969,575	6,245,936	42.6	47.5[a]

[a] The reduction in 1960 was due to the dropping of the merged General Motors companies (Motors and General Exchange) from the list of company groups. Without this
change the 1960 percentage would have been 49.4.

Source: Compiled from annual reports of automobile experience, *The National Underwriter*, 1950–1961.

One aspect of market structure which is not revealed in data
such as these is the fact that a number of companies which are small
nationally may be of considerable importance locally. This appears
to be the case particularly in parts of the Midwest and New England.
For example, the following companies earned the indicated percentage of *statewide* automobile bodily injury liability premiums in
1959: (1) Southern Farm Bureau Casualty, Arkansas, 11.6; (2)
Farm Bureau Mutual, Iowa, 10.9; (3) National Farmers Union,
North Dakota, 12.9; (4) Maine Bonding, Maine, 10.0; (5) Mer-
chants Mutual, New Hampshire, 10.6.[94] Although these 5 companies
averaged only $12 million in total earned premium for the year,[95]
each led all other insurers in the particular state.

While control of the automobile insurance business is now dis-
persed among several hundred companies, it is possible that the
number of insurers will be substantially reduced in future years.
The number of property-casualty company mergers by 5-year per-

[94] "Guide to Insurance Markets," *The Spectator*, Vol. CLXVIII (Nov. 1960), p. 79.
[95] *The National Underwriter*, June 10, 1960, pp. 27, ff.

TABLE 11—Automobile Insurance Earned Premium, Allstate Insurance Company and State Farm Mutual Automobile Insurance Company, Annually, 1949-1960

Year	Earned Premiums of:				Per Cent of Total		
	All-State	State Farm	All-state and State Farm[a]	All Companies	All-state	State Farm	All-state and State Farm[a]
	Thousand Dollars				%	%	%
1949	$ 40,905	$ 86,098	$127,003	$2,468,561	1.7	3.5	5.1
1950	49,642	95,511	145,153	2,547,242	1.9	3.7	5.7
1951	67,568	108,970	176,539	2,882,924	2.3	3.8	6.1
1952	89,232	126,320	215,552	3,333,799	2.7	3.8	6.5
1953	131,795	175,186	306,981	3,914,244	3.4	4.5	7.8
1954	171,946	201,392	373,337	4,181,339	4.1	4.8	8.9
1955	208,206	225,755	433,960	4,381,859	4.8	5.2	9.9
1956	236,274	263,778	500,052	4,580,585	5.2	5.8	10.9
1957	264,365	381,093	582,458	4,906,820	5.4	6.5	11.9
1958	297,811	369,826	667,636	5,308,959	5.6	7.0	12.6
1959	367,810	419,740	787,550	5,818,837	6.3	7.2	13.5
1960	425,381	455,660	881,041	6,245,936	6.8	7.3	14.1

[a] May not equal sum of components owing to rounding.

Source: Compiled from annual reports of automobile experience, *The National Underwriter*, 1950–1961.

iods beginning with 1940 has been 37, 55, 79, 175.[96] Some people expect to see the industry reduced to only 40 or 50 insurers in a decade or so.[97] The Senate subcommittee investigating the insurance business reported that "while relatively low concentration in the insurance business suggests that the merger movement has heretofore not been of dangerous proportions, all signs point to an accelerated pace in the future."[98]

CONDUCT OF THE MARKET

Nonprice Competition

Competition for automobile insurance, as for most other products, includes efforts by the sellers to obtain business on the basis of offering a lower price than that of rival companies, and on the

[96] Marryott, Franklin J., "Rate Regulation Revisited," *Insurance and Government* (The University of Wisconsin Insurance Series, Vol. II, No. 4; Madison, Wisconsin: Fund for Insurance Education and Research, 1960), p. 46.
[97] *The National Underwriter*, May 8, 1959, p. 43.
[98] *First Insurance Report*, p. 225.

basis of other appeals not directly involving price. This study deals specifically with price competition. However, as nonprice rivalry is also an important aspect of market conduct, an awareness of such competition is often pertinent to the regulation of price competition.[99]

Nonprice competition in automobile insurance includes attempts to secure business by means of appeal based on the following:

1. Policy coverage
2. Claim settlement service
3. Agency service
4. Agency type
5. Company type
6. Availability of other lines
7. Special policy package and payment plans
8. Advertising

Policy coverage was relatively standardized from 1936 until recent years as a result of the standard policy program adopted jointly by the major rating bureaus. In 1946 it was estimated that three-fourths of the automobile policies were written on the standard forms.[100] During the past few years variation in policy coverage has increasingly become an instrument of competition.[101]

The importance of claim settlement service as a competitive device is probably not great. Because superior claim service is advertised by all insurers, such assertions tend to cancel one another. One exception may be the advantage held by those companies which are able to offer country-wide claim service by their own employees or agents. Competition based upon agency service and the type of agency system employed is intense. As with rivalry based on company type however, it appears that much of this competition is more meaningful to the people in the insurance business than to prospective insurance buyers; this has been indicated by several consumer surveys.[102]

[99] To the extent that nonprice competition involves costs to the seller, the two forms of rivalry are alternatives and the company's price policy reflects its judgment of the optimum combination of price and nonprice competition.

[100] Kulp, C. A., *op. cit.*, p. 162.

[101] For example, State Farm claims "at least a dozen major fringe areas," in which its coverage exceeds that of the standard bureau form. *Insurance Hearings*, p. 1294.

[102] See Chapter II, Section on Significance of Price Competition.

Since most of the large automobile insurers are now multiple-line carriers, appeals based on the availability of other lines of coverage probably are important only in the competition between such companies and the smaller specialty insurers.

Innovations along such lines as installment-payment plans, six- and three-month policies, package policies (combining various coverages), and noncancellable insurance have come with increasing frequency in recent years. It is likely that they have often given important, although sometimes temporary, advantage to the innovating carrier.

The significance of advertising in insurance is somewhat limited due to the difficulty of creating public preference for the protection of one company over that of its competitors. Insurance service being both intangible and highly complex, the general public is not easily convinced by advertising which stresses such things as policy coverage or claim service. The advertising of the low-rate, direct-writers, however, has not been limited to abstractions; these companies have been able to concentrate on the premium saving available to their policy holders. The size of the advertising budgets[103] and the success of the direct writers in achieving rapid growth attest to the significance of this type of effort and also emphasize the relative importance of price competition in the automobile insurance market.

Price Competition

Extent of Price Competition—Throughout the history of property-casualty insurance in the United States rating bureaus and other company associations have attempted (with varying degrees of success) to control price competition.[104] In the automobile field self-regulation began almost with the development of the coverage,[105] forerunners of the three contemporary rating bureaus securing control of the bulk of the business at an early date.

A number of independent specialty companies entered the field in the 1920's to compete with the bureau companies. The specialty companies, many writing automobile coverages solely, used the

[103] It was estimated that the four leading direct-writers would spend more than $10 million for advertising in 1961. *The National Underwriter*, November 11, 1960, p. 20.
[104] See later, Chapter III.
[105] Wandel, William H., *op. cit.*, pp. 111–16.

American agency system but confined their operations to relatively small geographic areas. "The independent specialty company which could not compete with the conference company in terms of financial strength and security, competed with them by offering, first, a discount in rate, and, second, local personal service."[106] The rates charged by such companies were (and in many cases still are) typically a flat 10, 15 or 20 per cent reduction below bureau rates. In the 1920's there was sufficient "fat" in the bureau rates to permit such discounts by the specialty companies.[107] As competition continued through the 1920's and 1930's rates were driven downward forcing the low-rate companies to be more selective in their efforts to choose from among applicants for coverage.

> This screening process on the part of the cutrate companies naturally had the effect of leaving to the conference companies a higher proportion of undesirable risks than their rate making process anticipated. In this manner, not only the "fat" in the National Bureau and N.A.U.A. rates was completely cooked out but worse—the rates became inadequate for the average types of business written by the conference companies.[108]

Price competition by the independent specialty companies relied primarily upon reducing the loss ratio; their expense provisions, including commission allowance, differed little from those of the bureau companies. In the late 1940's the direct-writing companies began their spectacular advance.

> The attack of the direct writers was much more serious as now the Bureau companies had to meet competition not only on the loss ratio provision basis but also in their acquisition expense loading, something they had absolutely no control over. The direct writer, by eliminating the middleman or by reducing his cut of the premium, delivered what appeared to be a mortal blow to the conference companies.[109]

It is difficult, and perhaps impossible, to determine the exact difference in automobile insurance rates between the direct writers and the bureau companies. Each rate is based primarily upon the past experience of the particular state, and, to a lesser degree, of the rating territory within the state and the rating classification. Furthermore, there are minor differences among insurers in policy coverage, classification systems, and territorial definitions. The rate

106 Bell, S. Alexander, "Competition," *Best's Insurance News,* October 1954, p. 30.
107 *Ibid.*
108 *Ibid.*
109 *Ibid.,* p. 31.

differential therefore varies considerably.[110] For example, as of September 1957 the rates of Nationwide Mutual for specific rating classifications and territories ranged from 57 per cent to 105 per cent of National Bureau rates.[111]

Generalizations as to rate differentials therefore must be based upon the construction of rather complex rate indexes, the value of which is limited due to wide dispersion of rates from the average. An index of rates in force in September 1957 showed Nationwide rates ranging on a statewide basis from 65 per cent in Ohio to 85 per cent in New York of those charged by National Bureau companies. For the entire territory covered by Nationwide (at that time 15 states and the District of Columbia), its rates[112] were 25 per cent below the Bureau levels.[113] It is likely that Bureau company efforts to reduce expense ratios have narrowed this differential somewhat since 1957. Rates charged by the other leading direct writers are competitive with Nationwide's.

As previously stated, the direct-writing companies have been able to cut their rates by reducing the allowances for both company expenses and loss payments.

> In a letter to agents . . . Harold Evans, President of the American Casualty Company, cited figures to show that if the 75-cent premium dollar (on which the direct writing specialty companies operate on the average) is adjusted to a 100-cent dollar basis, it will be found that for the five years ending December 31, 1955, a representative group of . . . direct writers were able to operate at a 32 per cent savings as compared with a representative group of stock agency companies. . . . Total operating expenses (including commissions and taxes) of the direct writing companies were just half as much as those of the stock agency group. Furthermore, because of their practice of accepting only preferred business, the total loss and expense factor of the direct writers was 23 per cent less than the stock companies. As a consequence, while the stock companies over the five-year period . . . registered a 1 per cent operating gain, the non-agency companies, after providing a 25 per cent rate differential to policyholders, still ended up with a profit of 10 per cent.[114]

[110] See National Bureau, State Farm, Allstate and Nationwide liability rates by classification for the twenty-three Ohio territories. *Insurance Hearings,* pp. 4529–34.

[111] Crane, Frederick G., "Price Policy and Price Competition in Automobile Insurance," (Unpublished Master's thesis, The Ohio State University, 1957), p. 8.

[112] Excluding the "membership fee" charged only for the initial coverage period.

[113] Crane, Frederick G., *op. cit.,* p. 43.

[114] Kenney, Roger, "Critique of American Agency System," *Readings in Property and Casualty Insurance,* ed. Snider, H. Wayne (Homewood, Ill.: Richard D. Irwin, Inc., 1959), p. 272

The above analysis was summarized by Mr. Evans in the following manner:[115]

	Agency Companies	Direct Writers	Savings
Total operating expenses, including commissions and taxes			
(% of premiums written)	33%	22%	50% or
Cost per 100¢ dollar	33¢	16½¢	16½¢
Total loss and loss expense			
(% of premiums earned)	66%	68%	
Cost per 100¢ dollar	66¢	51¢	23% or 15¢
Total operating cost	99%	90%	32% or
Cost per 100¢ dollar	99¢	67½¢	31½¢

Tables 7 and 8 indicate that about one-half of the automobile premiums are written by Bureau members and subscribers, and one-half by nonbureau companies."[116] The proportions vary from state to state as do the rate differentials. Unfortunately, figures are not available to permit examination of the possible relationship between the two variables.[117] It does, however, appear reasonable to assume that both "the extent and intensity of intercompany rate competition in the various states is a function of several factors: (1) the number of insurance companies that desire to determine their own rates, (2) the provisions of the particular state statutes, (3) the regu-

[115] Kenney, Roger, "A Heart to Heart Talk to Agents on Future of the American Agency System," *United States Investor,* October 5, 1957, p. 25.

[116] It should be noted that such data exaggerate the relative importance of bureau writings because the non-bureau companies, writing at lower rates, must insure in excess of half of the vehicles in order to obtain half of the premium. See *Insurance Hearings,* p. 4938.

[117] The U. S. Senate investigating committee attempted to secure statistics showing the dollar volume of business written at bureau rates and the volume at less than bureau rates in each state, but found the effort to be "frustrating in the extreme." McHugh, Donald F., *op. cit.,* p. 109. All that it was able to obtain were approximate (and in some instances, rather questionable) percentages of this breakdown—and this from only 21 states. The percentages of automobile premiums written at full bureau rates in these states in 1957 reportedly ranged from 100 per cent in Texas to 10 per cent in Oregon. U. S., Congress, Senate, Subcommittee on Antitrust and Monopoly of the Committee on the Judiciary. *The Insurance Industry: Insurance: Rates, Rating Organizations and State Rate Regulation,* Report No. 831, 87th Congress, 1st Session, 1961, pp. 104–5. This report will hereafter be cited as "Second Insurance Report." The committee said that "a weighted statistical average used to estimate the mean percentage of the distributions" revealed that 49.8 per cent of automobile premiums were written at full bureau rates. *Ibid.,* p. 103. The committee stated that "replies in certain situations were suspect because of apparent differences in interpretation" and that "lack of complete and uniform records on rating activities and their competitive rating environment in many of the States diminished the value of many of the answers obtained." *Ibid.,* p. 80. Because of this and because no figures were submitted by certain key states, no further use of these data has been made in this study.

lations and orders of the insurance commissioner issued persuant to his interpretation of the statutes, (4) the courts' interpretation of the statutes, and (5) the extent and degree of the bureaus' opposition to such independent action."[118]

While competition between bureau and direct-writing companies is the most dramatic, price competition also takes place among the companies in each group. A number of individual bureau companies have adopted new rating plans and "economy" policy forms. To facilitate experimentation and innovation by its members the National Bureau has changed its regulations to permit individual companies to make such filings while retaining membership status.[119] Among nonbureau companies price competition is intense; the leading direct writers regard one another as their chief rivals.[120]

Currently, the inauguration of merit-rating plans (under which the premium level is affected by the driving record of the insured) is altering the nature of price competition. Such plans create more competition among bureau companies and among independent companies. Also, they bring bureau rates much nearer to, and sometimes below, the level of the direct writer's rates. This is particularly true when merit rating with a discount of up to 20 per cent is combined with an economy-type policy which provides a 15 to 20 per cent saving in its own right. Thus the bureau companies, faced with the loss of enormous amounts of automobile business to the direct writers since World War II, are attempting to strike back through the adoption of programs which will make their rates less uniform and more competitive.

In the current period of intensified competition the former pattern of dominance by a group of companies using standard rates, forms, and classification systems has largely broken down. This development, itself, is a significant factor of the automobile insurance market. Today's purchaser must choose, not between the standard product and a few minor variations, but among a huge array of prices, forms, and services.

[118] Dirlam, Joel B., and Stelzer, Irwin M., "The Insurance Industry: A Case Study in the Workability of Regulated Competition," *University of Pennsylvania Law Service*, Vol. CVII, No. 2 (December 1958), p. 205.

[119] *The National Underwriter*, March 24, 1961, p. 35.

[120] Testimony of Thomas C. Morrill, Vice President, State Farm Mutual Automobile Insurance Co., *Insurance Hearings*, p. 1304.

Effect of Selective Underwriting—Automobile insurance rating classifications, which categorize insureds according to such characteristics as age, mileage and use of the car, are "broad bands of hazard; each one with a wide spectrum of good and bad risks."[121] In other words, the risks within a given classification, each of which must be insured for the same premium, are not a perfectly homogeneous group; "the insurer cannot equate the desirability of risks in terms of their rates."[122] This gives rise to an important modification in the nature of price competition.

> . . . a risk is redundantly rated ("cream business") if it lies above the average of its rating category. It is "substandard" if it lies below. So insurers spend a vast amount of time, energy and money in trying to attract the "cream business" and trying to avoid the "substandard business."[123]

The American agency system companies using bureau rates have been handicapped in this competition for the best risks because of (1) occasional pressure from their independent agents to accept undesirable business (under threat of loss of good business to competing companies), (2) frequent necessity of writing a poor automobile risk in order to retain other lines of coverage written for the same insured, and (3) price competition from the direct writers. The price differential has been particularly devastating in this regard. It is an axiom in insurance that "lower rates improve selection." The National Bureau expressed the problem in the following manner:

> Unless our companies can revise their methods and operations to a point where they can be reasonably competitive as to price for the business which is also being sought by direct writers and reduced rate companies, the automobile liability insurance business of National Bureau companies is likely to be characterized by successive rounds of (1) increasing rate levels being offset by (2) a deterioration in the cross-section of business written previously resulting in (3) underwriting losses requiring (4) further rate increases and so forth.[124]

Another aspect of this problem is that the rating system may encourage continual refinement of the classifications as a competitive

---

[121] *The National Underwriter*, December 25, 1959, p. 25.

[122] Otto, Ingolf H. B., *op. cit.*, p. 208.

[123] Otto, Ingolf H. B., "Capacity," *Journal of Insurance*, Vol. XXVIII, No. 1 (March 1961), p. 59.

[124] Unpublished report of the National Bureau of Casualty Underwriters, July 15, 1953. It should be noted that since this report was written the bureaus and the bureau companies have in fact been revising their methods and operations in order to become more competitive in price.

device. To illustrate, if most companies are grouping all risks in the $40 to $60 range into a single classification and charging them a $50 rate, a maverick company may divide the category into two classifications. It may establish a $45 rate for those in the $40 to $50 range and a $55 rate for the $50 to $60 range. For the innovator, such a move would accomplish two things: it would facilitate its attempts to secure the "cream business" of the $40 to $60 classification, and it would permit the charging of a more adequate rate for the "substandard" risks which, in the absence of any classification system, would be charged rates ranging from $50 to $60. While the bureau companies use a system of 7 or 9 classifications in most states, some of the independents use as many as 35 or 40, leading the former group to urge insurance commissioners to limit the number of permissible rating categories.[125] It appears likely that this will become an increasing problem to the supervisory authorities as future technological advances increase the ability of underwriters to spot loss-producing characteristics in prospective insureds and to refine their classification accordingly.

The increasing selectivity of underwriting has had the side effect of increasing the population of the assigned risk pools. These provide limited liability coverage for persons whom the companies are not willing to insure voluntarily. The assigned risk pools in 1958 earned in excess of $100 million in premiums, which was over 3 per cent of the insurance business total.[126]

As long as the classification rating system is used, regardless of the number of classes employed and whatever the rate level approved by the state, insurers will compete strongly for the best risks, hoping to reject those which will produce more than the class average of losses.

Unfair Price Competition—Most of the price competition in this market is in the open, being based upon rate filings approved by the state insurance department. However, an indeterminant, but probably substantial,[127] amount falls in the category of secret and "unfair" competition.

[125] Evans, Harold G., "The Auto Insurance Dilemma," *Best's Insurance News,* January 1960, p. 22.
[126] Isaacs, Edgar E., "Undesirable Automobile Risks," *Best's Insurance News,* February 1961, p. 65.
[127] Kimball, Spencer L., and Jackson, Bartlett, *op. cit.,* p. 199.

Each of the states has enacted the substance of a Model Unfair Trade Practices Act as proposed by the National Association of Insurance Commissioners. Besides outlawing unfair competition in general, the statutes forbid several specific practices such as misrepresentation, false advertising, unfair discrimination, and rebating.[128] The Senate investigating committee reported that the states have not been diligent in enforcing these requirements.[129]

The most prevalent type of unfair price competition in automobile insurance is the intentional misclassification of the risks insured. This sometimes is done in order to reduce the rate below that of competitors.[130] "The temptation on the part of a commission agent to obtain business by rate cutting is one which human nature is ill fitted to withstand, and the companies are much too dependent upon their agency connections to exercise effective restraint."[131] Risks also have been misclassified in order to increase the rate. Investigations by federal and state officials in 1957 and 1958 led to estimates of overcharges of up to $25 million by physical damage insurers. As a result, over $10 million was refunded to policyholders, principally by insurers affiliated with sales finance companies.[132]

An even more serious problem to insurance regulators is the alleged use of loss leaders. This is involved in the American agency system—direct-writer dispute, the former companies charging that "the direct writers make it a practice of filing cut rates in order to obtain business and then after they have the business make a subsequent filing increasing the rate."[133] The direct-writing companies deny that this is done,[134] while the regulators face the problem of preserving fair competition whatever may be the truth of the opposing arguments.

Significance of Price Competition—It has been seen that there is intensive price competition among automobile insurers. One might still ask, however, whether this is important. Are people aware of

---

[128] *Ibid.*, p. 143.

[129] *First Insurance Report,* p. 239.

[130] For a specific allegation of such practice, see *Insurance Hearings,* p. 1867.

[131] Downey, E. H., "The Public Supervision of Workmen's Compensation Insurance," *Modern Insurance Problems* (Philadelphia: The American Academy of Political and Social Science, 1917), p. 312.

[132] Rokes, Willis P., *op. cit.,* p. 163.

[133] *Insurance Hearings,* p. 2789.

[134] *Ibid.,* p. 1245.

the price differentials, and do they buy automobile insurance on the basis of price? Motivations, of course, differ among purchasers. Many persons select an insurance agent rather than a company, perhaps because he is a relative or customer. Some people are influenced by the recommendations of friends or parents. To many, the reputation of a company for service is more important than price.

It is always dangerous to generalize about consumer motivations, but available evidence does seem to point to price as the most important single criterion in the selection of an automobile insurer. Several consumer surveys have indicated that a large but decreasing percentage of automobile policy holders believe that all companies charge about the same price.[135] An extensive survey by the National Bureau in 1956 revealed that 43 per cent believed this was the case.[136] Knowledge of this lack of consumer information touched off massive rate advertising campaigns by the low-rate companies, undoubtedly increasing consumer awareness of price differences.

In other surveys automobile policyholders have been asked why they selected their particular company. The consensus has been that consumers consider price more important than things like company type and reputation or even company service.[137] According to the National Bureau study this was true of those insured both with low-rate and with standard-rate companies. Seven of 10 of the latter group believed they were paying the lowest possible rates,[138] a point which emphasized the vulnerability of the bureau companies to price advertising by the direct writers.

Additional evidence of the significance of price is found in the success of the low-rate companies. Table 11 showed that the premium earnings of State Farm and Allstate have increased to 14.1 per cent of the total. Assuming a rate level 20 per cent below bureau prices, it has been calculated that these two, and two other direct writers (Nationwide and Farmers Insurance Exchange) have saved automobile policyholders in excess of $1 billion during the past five years.[139] Coupled with the findings of the consumer surveys, the

---

135 Crane, Frederick G., op. cit., pp. 59–61.
136 The National Underwriter, August 22, 1957, p. 4.
137 Crane, Frederick G., op. cit., pp. 61–68.
138 The National Underwriter, loc. cit.
139 Bell, S. Alexander, "Independents' Experience," Best's Insurance News, June 1960, p. 109

fact that these companies have captured an increasing proportion of the market while the bureau-rate companies' share has declined strengthens the belief that price is the dominant criterion in the purchase of automobile insurance.[140] Such an indication further underscores the importance of price regulation in this field.

[140] Of course, opinions differ as to whether or not price *should be* the dominant criterion. See discussion earlier in this chapter.

CHAPTER III

THE INSTRUMENTS OF CONTROL AND THEIR DEVELOPMENT

THE CONTROL OF PRICE COMPETITION BEFORE THE McCARRAN ACT

The concept that insurance practices are properly subject to government supervision developed almost simultaneously with the emergence of insurance as a business institution.[1] The first known regulation of insurance prices by a special public agency was enacted in Florence (now in Italy) in 1523. Rate fixing authority was granted to commissioners "provided they conform themselves to equitable regulations in the matter."[2]

Establishment of State Laws and Departments

Effective insurance supervision was slow to develop in the United States. In the early years of the country, government action was largely confined to the chartering of companies. The first insurance statues were perhaps those passed by Pennsylvania and South Carolina in 1810 prohibiting the writing of insurance in their states by foreign companies.[3]

The first insurance commissioner was appointed by New Hampshire in 1850. Two years later, commissioners or boards were designated in 7 additional states.[4] In 1859 New York became the first state to have an executive department devoted solely to insurance supervision.[5]

[1] Magee, John H., *General Insurance*, 5th ed. (Homewood, Illinois: Richard D. Irwin, Inc., 1957), p. 918.

[2] Patterson, Edwin W., *op. cit.*, p. 515. Patterson adds that "modern rate-fixing statutes have added but little to this formula in the way of exactness."

[3] *In the Public Interest: One Hundred Years of Insurance Supervision in New York State* (New York: Insurance Industry Committee for the New York Insurance Department Centennial, 1960), p. 10.

[4] *Insurance Hearings*, p. 4840.

[5] *In the Public Interest . . . loc. cit.*, p. 12.

Initially, the Department was given only limited powers, hardly more effective than those previously exercised by the State Comptroller. Early supervision was almost solely directed toward disclosing the financial condition of fire insurance companies. It was only later that the jurisdiction of the Department was extended to life and marine companies. Its functions, chiefly, were: 1) to prescribe the form of annual statement to be used by the companies; 2) to be the custodian of securities required to be deposited by life insurance companies; and 3) to examine the insurance companies' books at their home offices whenever it was considered necessary.[6]

The constitutionality of state laws regulating insurance was challenged in a case which reached the Supreme Court in 1868.[7] The case involved Samuel Paul, a Virginia insurance agent who represented several New York companies and who refused to comply with a Virginia statute requiring the deposit of securities on behalf of nonresident insurers. Paul argued that the insurance business was commerce and in this case was interstate commerce. Paul claimed that since the Constitution reserves control over interstate commerce to Congress, the Virginia statute was unconstitutional. The court rejected Paul's contention, stating that "issuing a policy of insurance is not a transaction of commerce. . . . The policies . . . are . . . local transactions, and are governed by the local law."[8] This position of the Court was upheld in a number of subsequent cases in following years.[9]

After the Paul case, additional states established insurance laws and departments. By 1890 authorities were supervising insurance in 17 states.[10] The degree of regulation varied widely among them, various forms of supervision being enacted piecemeal. New York, for example, did not establish a general insurance law until 1892.[11] None of the states were at this time regulating insurance prices.

The Compact System and Anti-Compact Laws

Walton Hamilton has described the "government of industry" existing apart from the ordinary operations of state, but which "in its own distinctive way has its constitution and its statutes, its ad-

[6] Ibid.
[7] Paul v. Virginia, 8 Wall. 168.
[8] Ibid., p. 183.
[9] See Sawyer, Elmer W., Insurance as Interstate Commerce (New York: McGraw-Hill, 1945), p. 40 for citation of 11 such cases.
[10] Ibid., p. 38.
[11] In the Public Interest . . . loc. cit., p. 19.

ministrative and judicial processes, and its own manner of dealing with those who do not abide by the law of the industry."[12] "The impulse to get together is strong," he states, "for as an unleashed force competition is hazardous. There must be rules for the game or business mortality will run high, and survival and security are urges which are ever present."[13]

Probably nowhere in industry is the impulse to get together stronger than in the insurance business. Throughout the history of insurance regulation one of the major issues facing supervisory officials has been whether the elimination of price competition through cooperative action should be prevented, condoned, or enforced.

The Compact System—The effects of unrestrained price competition became apparent early in the history of the American fire insurance business. "The existence of the evils attending inter-company conflicts, the penalties for which are levied upon the insuring public as well as upon the companies themselves, has been recognized from the beginning of these conflicts, and has resulted in an almost uninterrupted history of attempts to control competition."[14]

> Losses seemed to follow cyclical patterns. A low loss ratio and high profits attracted newcomers by the prospect of quick riches. Insurance companies were easy to start, for a rented office, a few clerks, and some solicitors on commission would suffice. Moreover, if it did not set up adequate reinsurance reserves, a new company would enjoy an illusion of large profits even if the business were potentially insolvent, since the delay from premium payment to claims payment meant that income of even an unsound company would greatly exceed outgo so long as the business was expanding. Hence, the frequently excessive competition forced premiums down to uneconomic levels and ultimately drove companies out of existence.[15]

At least as early as 1819 local associations were formed to control price competition in fire insurance.[16] From then until 1866 many such attempts were made, but with little success, as rate cutting continued and many companies failed.[17]

In 1866 the National Board of Fire Underwriters was formed, one of its purposes being "to establish and maintain, as far as prac-

---

[12] Hamilton, Walton, *Politics of Industry* (New York: Alfred A. Knopf, 1957), p. 7.
[13] *Ibid.*, p. 8.
[14] Wandel, William H., *op. cit.*, p. 15.
[15] Kimbell, Spencer L., *Insurance and Public Policy* (Madison: University of Wisconsin Press, 1960), p. 94.
[16] Wandel, William H., *op. cit.*, p. 15.
[17] *Insurance Hearings*, p. 4360.

ticable, a system of uniform rates of premium."[18] For a few years the National Board exercised rate jurisdiction over local boards and agents. However, the disastrous Chicago fire of 1871, the Boston fire of 1872 and the panic of 1873 hit the industry hard, causing many companies to fail. The surviving companies cut their rates in an effort to secure increased revenue.[19] Finally, in 1877 the National Board was forced to abandon its efforts at rate making and rate maintenance.

In the 1880's the compact system developed. This provided for the making and maintenance of rates by a local compact manager under the jurisdiction of regional company associations. Assisting in the maintenance of the agreed-upon rates were stamping offices which checked a copy of each fire policy issued by compact members.[20]

Anti-Compact Laws—The main difficulty in the various attempts at self-regulation was the maintenance of membership discipline and the policing of the regulations established by the associations;[21] there was little concern with the propriety of stifling competition.[22] The period around the turn of the century, however, was one of intense anti-monopoly agitation. Not surprisingly, some of this feeling focused upon the pricing practices of insurance companies. Beginning with Ohio and New Hampshire in 1885, a number of states enacted anti-compact legislation. Such laws, prohibiting membership in associations which fixed or maintained premium rates, were passed by 23 states betwen 1885 and 1912.[23]

The industry showed considerable ingenuity in escaping the intended force of the anti-compact laws. In some cases the laws applied only to companies incorporated in the particular state, or only to companies and not to agents; evasion was simple in these instances. In other states the laws applied to all companies and agents;

---

[18] *Proceedings,* National Board of Fire Underwriters, July 19, 1866, p. 14. Quoted in Wandel, William H., *op. cit.,* p. 18.

[19] Stelzer, I. M., "The Insurance Industry and the Anti-trust Laws," *Insurance Law Journal,* No. 386 (March 1955), p. 141.

[20] Wandel, William H., *op. cit.,* p. 51.

[21] *Ibid.,* pp. 89–124.

[22] Moser, Henry S., "Competition and Insurance," *Insurance Law Journal,* No. 384 (May 1955), p. 306.

[23] *U. S.* v. *South-Eastern Underwriters Association,* 322 U. S. 540, n. 43, 1944.

these were more of a challenge to the industry, resulting in such devices as secret meetings and code messages, or the sale of rate-making
services by "independent" bureaus.[24] To the extent that the anti-
compact laws were effective, cooperative rating had to be abandoned.

Establishment of Rate Regulatory Laws

The first law to regulate property-casualty rates was adopted by
Kansas in 1909. It required companies to file their rates with the
insurance commissioner and authorized him to order any revisions
necessary to prevent the use of excessive or inadequate rates.[25]

During the next few years investigating committees in several
states considered the adoption of statutes regulating insurance pricing as an alternative to anti-compact legislation. There was general
agreement by these committees on the advisability of permitting
joint rate making.[26]

The most influential of the investigations was that conducted
in 1910 and 1911 by the Merritt Committee in New York.[27] Its
recommendations were followed by several states and its report
is regarded by many people as being authoritative even today.

Concentrating upon fire insurance, the Merritt Committee urged
that New York adopt the rate regulatory approach rather than en-
act anti-compact legislation.[28] The Committee said that anti-compact
laws were aimed at insurance "trusts,"[29] but that combinations of
insurance companies were not trusts because there was competition
among the members of the combinations.[30] Anyway, the anti-trust
laws were easily evaded[31] and did not bring about a state of open
competition.[32] Regarding open competition, the Committee report
added:

[24] Wandel, William H., *op. cit.*, pp. 127–133.
[25] Hobbs, Clarence W., "State Regulation of Insurance Rates," *Proceedings of the
Casualty Actuarial Society*, Vol. XI, No. 24 (June 1925), p. 221.
[26] National Convention of Insurance Commissioners, *Proceedings*, 1915, pp. 119–144.
[27] State of New York, *Report of the Joint Committee of the Senate and Assembly of
the State of New York Appointed to Investigate Corrupt Practices in Connection with Legislation, and the Affairs of Insurance Companies, Other Than Those Doing a Life Insurance
Business*, Assembly Document No. 30, 134th Sess. (1911). The *Report* is quoted in *Insurance
Hearings*, pp. 2791–2882. Citations below are from that source.
[28] *Ibid.*, p. 2858.
[29] *Ibid.*, p. 2806.
[30] *Ibid.*, p. 2821.
[31] *Ibid.*, p. 2806.
[32] *Ibid.*, p. 2827.

> It is not necessary to theorize about this for there is plenty of evidence in the rate wars which were formerly carried on and which to some degree still prevail. The universal effect of such periods of open competition wherever and whenever they have occurred has been a cutting of rates to a point that was below the actual cost of the indemnity. If the rate war had been general this would have meant the ultimate death of the company, and rate wars of even a local character lead, if long continued, to the dissolution of the smaller and weaker companies. The effect on all companies is weakening. The policyholder, to be sure, gets his insurance very cheaply; too cheaply, for the weakening of the companies is not in the long run and on the whole an economic good, for there is just so much less protection behind the insured . . .[33]

The Merritt Committee noted the desirability of rates based upon the pooled experience of many companies.[34] But it is stated that "the present situation wherein rate making exchanges and associations wield a power which properly belongs to government should be ended."[35] Rejecting State rate making as a solution,[36] the Committee recommended instead that "a statute be enacted that will permit combination under State regulation."[37]

Later in the same year (1911), New York adopted legislation of the type favored by the Merritt Committee. Rate-making associations were authorized but were required to file rates with the state insurance commissioner and to operate under his general supervision.[38]

In 1914, the Supreme Court upheld the constitutionality of state insurance rate regulation. The case concerned the Kansas law under which a reduction in fire insurance rates had been ordered by the commissioner. The Court ruled that the insurance business is sufficiently affected with a public interest to justify state regulation, adding:

> We may venture to observe that the price of insurance is not fixed over the counters of the companies by what Adam Smith calls the higgling of the market, but formed in the councils of the underwriters, promulgated

[33] Ibid., p. 2804.

[34] Ibid.

[35] Ibid., p. 2858.

[36] Ibid., p. 2828.

[37] Ibid., p. 2858.

[38] Collins, Joseph F., "Rate Regulation in Fire and Casualty Insurance," Examination of Insurance Companies (Vol. V; New York: New York State Insurance Department, 1955), p. xviii.

in schedules of practically controlling constancy which the applicant for insurance is powerless to oppose and which, therefore, has led to the assertion that the business of insurance is of monopolistic character and that "it is illusory to speak of a liberty of contract."[39]

A committee of the National Convention of Insurance Commissioners in 1914 recommended passage of state laws authorizing and regulating rate bureaus.[40] In the following years additional states adopted such legislation.

The scope and effectiveness of rate regulation differed among the states. Since the legislation in many instances resulted from distrust of fire insurance companies and the suspicion that fire rates were too high, regulation often concentrated on this line of coverage and upon rate excessiveness. Other types of insurance and rate adequacy were given less attention.[41] In many instances the early laws never accomplished their intended purpose. In Wisconsin, for example, the legislature applied rate regulation to liability insurance in 1919 and yet it is said that supervision was not truly effective until the 1950's.[42]

By 1944, 33 states had some form of rate regulatory machinery,[43] 10 of them requiring the filing and approval of automobile insurance rates.[44] Fifteen states had taken no action other than to pass anti-compact or general anti-monopoly laws.[45] "In the casualty field before 1944, there was no crystallized regulatory pattern. . . . Except in the field of workmen's compensation, most of the states did not subject casualty rates to any more pervasive regulation than prohibitions against discrimination."[46] "Though ostensibly there was control in two-thirds of the states, insurance rate making was as yet largely uncontrolled in the United States."[47]

[39] *German Alliance Insurance Company* v. *Lewis, 233* U. S. 389, 416 (1914).

[40] National Convention of Insurance Commissioners, *Proceedings,* 1914, p. 19.

[41] Hobbs, Clarence W., "State Regulation of Insurance Rates," *Proceedings of the Casualty Actuarial Society,* Vol. XXVIII, No. 58 (May 1942), p. 346 and 401.

[42] Kimball, Spencer L., *op. cit.,* p. 108.

[43] Kimball, Spencer L., and Boyce, Ronald N., "The Adequacy of State Insurance Rate Regulation," Michigan Law Review, Vol. LVI, No. 4 (February 1958), p. 552.

[44] Moser, Henry S., "Operation of Independents Under the Rate Regulatory Pattern," *Law and Contemporary Problems,* Vol. 15, No. 4 (Autumn 1950), p. 526.

[45] Kimball, Spencer L. and Boyce, Ronald N., *loc. cit.*

[46] Moser, Henry S., *loc. cit.*

[47] Kimball, Spencer L., and Boyce, Ronald N., *loc. cit.* For similar comment by the National Association of Insurance Commissioners, see *Insurance Hearings,* pp. 4872–3.

South-Eastern Underwriters Association Case

State regulation had developed since 1868 on the basis of the *Paul* v. *Virginia* ruling that insurance was not commerce and hence not within the jurisdiction of Congress. In 1944, that ruling was upset.[48]

The South-Eastern Underwriters Association is a fire insurance rating bureau. In 1944 it had nearly 200 member companies and controlled 90 per cent of the fire business in its territory. The Association was indicted for violations of the Sherman Antitrust Act, being charged with conspiracy to monopolize trade.

Reversing its previous doctrine,[49] the Court in this case ruled that insurance was commerce and that its inter-state aspects were therefore subject to Congressional control. The decision was highly disturbing to the insurance industry because

> . . . the federal anti-trust laws—as the Supreme Court construed them—forbade all price-fixing agreements between business competitors and thus seemed to threaten to return to the evils of unrestrained competition in premiums for fire insurance, which it was thought had been exorcised a generation before. . . . The situation was further complicated by an anxiety lest the decision that insurance was interstate commerce have the effect of invalidating the system of state regulation and supervision already built up.[50]

THE McCARRAN ACT AND THE ALL-INDUSTRY LAWS

The McCarran Act

The dilemma created by the South-Eastern Underwriters Association case, with insurance rate making and state regulation suddenly in conflict with federal law, was quickly resolved by Congressional passage of the McCarran Act.[51] Adopted in 1945, the Act declared that continued regulation and taxation of insurance by the states is in the public interest. The federal antitrust acts are made applicable to insurance "to the extent that such business is not regulated by State law," with the exception that the Sherman Act continues to apply to boycott, coercion and intimidation.

[48] *U. S.* v. *South-Eastern Underwriters Association,* 322 U. S. 533.

[49] Actually, this was the first case in which federal control was an issue. The previous cases had concerned only the validity of state regulation.

[50] Gardner, George K., "Insurance and the Antitrust Laws," *Harvard Law Review,* Vol. LXI (January 1948), p. 259.

[51] Public Law No. 15, 79th Congress, 1st Sess. (1945).

In signing the McCarran Act President Roosevelt stated:

> . . . the Anti-Trust Laws and certain related statutes will be applicable in
> full force and effect to the business of insurance except to the extent that
> the States have assumed the responsibility for the regulation of whatever
> aspect of the insurance business may be involved. . . . Congress did not
> intend to permit private rate fixing, which the Anti-Trust Act forbids;
> but was willing to permit actual regulation of rates by affirmative action
> of these states.[52]

In preference to the antitrust principle, Congress thus established
as national policy state control of jointly made insurance rates.

The All-Industry Bills

In order to keep the federal antitrust statutes inapplicable to
insurance, it was necessary for the states to revise their laws if they
did not effectively and affirmatively regulate the business. Attention
of the states was immediately directed at rate regulation, as uncontrolled joint price fixing was obviously in conflict with the federal
laws.[53]

An All-Industry Committee was organized consisting of representatives from 19 national insurance organizations.[54] This group,
together with the National Association of Insurance Commissioners,
drafted model rate regulatory bills which were recommended to the
states.[55]

The All-Industry Casualty and Surety Rate Regulatory Bill (hereafter referred to as the All-Industry Bill) permits rates to be made
either jointly or independently. It requires that they be filed with
the state insurance department in either case. The rates are subject
to disapproval by the insurance commissioner within a 15- or 30-day
waiting period. Specific sections of the bill reflect adherence by its
draftees to the following statement of purposes:

1. It is the intent of Congress that provision should be made in the State
   regulatory structure for companies acting individually and for companies acting in concert.

[52] *Insurance Hearings*, p. 4879.

[53] The Court had repeatedly held that price fixing was illegal *per se*, even when the
price fixed was lower than an independently determined price would have been. See *U. S.*
v. Socony Vacuum Oil Co., 310 U. S. 150 and cases cited.

[54] For a list of the organizations see *Insurance Hearings*, p. 4882.

[55] The bills were approved by the N.A.I.C. June 12, 1946, *Ibid.*, p. 4886. Separate rate
bills were proposed for (1) Fire, Marine and Inland Marine and (2) Casualty and Surety.
See Note 2, above, Chapter I.

2. To insure competition, the quasi-public character of rating bureaus should be recognized and the proposed bills should contain provisions for their licensing and supervision and also for examination and visitation.

3. The bill should provide for the freest possible use of bureau facilities by both members and subscribers and unfairly restrictive bureau rules should be eliminated.

4. Rates should not be excessive, inadequate, unfairly discriminatory or otherwise unreasonable whether filed by independent companies or by companies acting in concert.

5. The legislation should not make it compulsory for any insurance company to become a member of rating bureaus or to charge uniform rates.[56]

Price competition is made possible by provisions which permit (1) bureau rate filings, (2) deviations from bureau filings, (3) direct filings by independent companies, and (4) dividends by either bureau or independent companies.

Adoption of the All-Industry Laws

The threat of federal intervention "shook state supervision out of complacency, forced it to engage in a painful process of self-analysis, and galvanized it into remedial action."[57] During 1947 new rate laws or revisions of existing laws were adopted in 37 jurisdictions, the remaining ones following suit soon after.[58]

Several alternatives to the All-Industry type of regulation were considered. The other proposals included (1) regulation of cooperatively made rates only, other rates to be free of supervision; (2) regulation confined to maximum rates, lower rates to be free of supervision; (3) elimination of rate filing requirements; (4) cooperative rating confined to determination of the pure premium (i.e., the amount of premium necessary to pay losses), insurers being free to fix expenses and profit loadings; (5) mandatory bureau membership for all companies with rate deviations limited to uniform percentage changes.[59]

Selection of the All-Industry formula represented a compromise between the advocates of strict control and those who favored a

---

[56] *Insurance Hearings*, p. 4887.
[57] *In the Public Interest . . . op. cit.*, p. 35.
[58] *Insurance Hearings*, p. 4893.
[59] Dineen, Robert E., "The AIC Bills and The Alternatives," *Journal of American Insurance*, Vol. XXIII (November 1946), pp. 29–31; Williams, C. Arthur, *op. cit.*, pp. 48–54.

more liberal approach. In the former group were the state officials and dividend-paying mutuals. Many bureau and independent companies favored less control.[60]

The rate regulatory laws of almost all of the states are today patterned after the model bills recommended by the National Association of Insurance Commissioners and the All-Industry Committee. Although there are minor modifications in these laws,[61] they reflect the All-Industry interpretation of the proper balance between uniform and competitive rate making. In a few states, the All-Industry pattern was not followed and the laws aim at achieving a markedly different degree of price competition.[62]

STATE RATE SUPERVISION

The Insurance Departments and Commissioners

Reference has already been made to the great and diverse responsibilities of state insurance regulators.[63]

In Patterson's words,

. . . sometimes the insurance commissioner is an official clerk, sometimes he is a judge, sometimes he is a law-giver, and sometimes he is both prosecuting attorney and hangman. He is partly executive, partly judicial and partly legislative; and yet he is not confined within any of these categories.[64]

A striking characteristic of insurance regulators is the apparent diversity in their ability to perform their many duties effectively. In some states a well qualified, highly paid commissioner has a huge corps of technicians to assist him in carrying out the responsibilities of the department. In some other instances the opposite appears to be the case.

The commissioner[65] is appointed in 40 jurisdictions, elected in 11, and in one state is selected by competitive civil service examination.[66] His term of office is indefinite in 11 states and ranges down to two

[60] Williams, C. Arthur, *loc. cit.;* Brook, Herbert C., "Public Interest and the Commissioners'—All-Industry Laws," *Law and Contemporary Problems,* Vol. XV, No. 4 (Autumn 1950), pp. 607–610.

[61] For a detailed analysis of the differences, see Carlson, Thomas O., *op. cit.*

[62] See Chapter IV.

[63] Above, Chapter I.

[64] Patterson, Edwin W., *op. cit.,* p. 5.

[65] Or "superintendent" or "director." See *First Insurance Report,* p. 112, Note 12.

[66] *Ibid.,* p. 114.

years in 6 others.[67] He is paid a salary of $20,000 in Texas and $18,500 in New York, but in Delaware and North Dakota must be willing to accept the position for only $6,000.[68] In 1957 the total budget of the New York Insurance Department was well over $4 million while 31 states operated with less than $200 thousand, and 18 states managed with less than $100 thousand.[69] In the same year, the New York department had a staff of 583 persons; Texas had 370; Massachusetts, 239, and California, 231. At least 17 states ran their insurance departments with a staff of under 20 persons, while in 7 states the commissioner had less than 10 on his staff, including clerical workers.[70]

One result of these disparities has been reliance by many of the states upon the lead of a few states like New York, particularly in the development of new legislation and other matters beyond the scope of routine supervision.[71] The less affluent departments have also been assisted by the National Association of Insurance Commissioners, whose many committees study specific regulatory problems as they arise and recommend appropriate action. The Association also provides a means of interstate cooperation in the examination of insurance companies.[72]

Rate Regulatory Procedures

Automobile insurance rate revisions are usually filed with the state insurance departments by the rating organizations and the independent companies each year. The filings are accompanied by supporting information including detailed statistical experience by class and territory. In Carlson's opinion the adequacy of the supporting information "probably constitutes the most difficult single problem of the supervisory official."[73] In this regard the All-Industry laws say:

> The information furnished in support of a filing may include (1) the experience or judgment of the insurer or rating organization making the

[67] *Ibid.*, p. 118.
[68] *Ibid.*, p. 127.
[69] *Ibid.*, p. 152.
[70] *Ibid.*, pp. 138–9.
[71] Kenney, Roger, "Legislative Protection of Commisisons Has Dangerous Ends for American Agency System," *United States Investor,* March 20, 1961, p. 42.
[72] The history and functions of the Association are described in *Insurance Hearings,* pp. 4839–66.
[73] Carlson, Thomas D., *op. cit.,* p. 20.

filing, (2) its interpretation of any statistical data it relies upon, (3) the experience of other insurers or rating organizations, or (4) any other relevant factors.[74]

It is seen that the laws permit the submission in support of a filing of anything that appears to be relevant. Any of the four items listed above may be included, but no particular one is mandatory except as required by the commissioner on the basis of his own judgment. "Thus although the supervisory official does not have the authority to make rates, any filing which in his *judgment* does not meet the statutory requirements may be, indeed must be, disapproved."[75]

The requirement that rates be neither "excessive, inadequate or unfairly discriminatory" applies both to bureau rates and those of independent companies. When the filings of independent or deviating companies call for rate levels different from bureau rates such differentials are usually justified on the basis of expense savings by the non-bureau companies. Rate differences are less often granted on grounds of more favorable loss experience.[76]

Detailed consideration is normally given by the state officials to each factor entering into the determination of revised rates. Frequently this includes informal discussions and correspondence with the filer. If the filing is acceptable to the insurance department it is placed on file, and the companies distribute revised manual pages to their agents.

The framers of the All-Industry laws felt that casualty insurance in 1946 was in a state of flux which made it impossible to anticipate the changes which would become desirable. For that reason they felt it best "to establish principles of regulation within which administrative authority can exercise a broad discretionary power, rather than to set forth details which, under changed conditions, might stand in the way of desirable developments in rate making."[77]

[74] Section 4. See *Insurance Hearings*, p. 5009.

[75] Resony, John A., "Discussion of 'Rate Regulation and the Casualty Actuary,'" *Proceedings of the Casualty Actuarial Society*, Vol. XXXVIII, No. 70 (November 1951), p. 225. (Emphasis in original.)

[76] *Insurance Hearings*, p. 1797.

[77] All-Industry Committee, *Casualty and Surety Rate-Regulatory Bill, Explanatory Memorandum*, October 23, 1946. Quoted in Kulp, C. A., *op. cit.*, p. 576. The flexibility of the laws and vagueness of the rate standards have led to proposals for revision to make them "specific enough to state a legal method which, if followed, would produce a set of rates that could not be defeated just because the commissioner says that in his judgment the

There is no doubt that the framers succeeded in providing the flexibility they desired; a perhaps unintended result has been the differences in interpretation of the laws which inevitably arose.

OBJECTIVES OF RATE REGULATION

Although application of the rate laws differs among the states, there appears to be general agreement, for the most part, on the basic objectives of rate regulation.

The declared purpose of the All-Industry laws is "to promote the public welfare."[78] The "public" is widely interpreted to mean policyholders and claimants primarily. The private welfare of any person or company, or of any group of persons or companies is of only secondary concern.[79] Thus the principal purpose is not to promote or preserve the status of any type of company or any type of agency system, nor is the convenience of the administering authority an essential feature of insurance regulation. The nature of the public interest served by rate regulation is eloquently described in the following statement:

> Insurance affects the lives, property, welfare and security of a large part of the total population. Insurance takes small amounts of premium from great numbers of people for the benefit of the few who are struck by catastrophe. Insurance, through the safeguarding and investment of funds in effect held in trust for claimants, exercises a tremendous influence upon the economic life and organization of the country. Insurance contracts are complicated legal documents, the interpretation and evaluation of which are entirely outside the scope of ordinary activities of most insurance buyers. Manifestly, it is greatly in the public interest that the public be able to buy such contracts easily, that the public can rely on the contract without legal advice, that the price charged for the protection of the contract be fair, reasonable and not excessive, that all buyers are treated alike without unfair discrimination, and above all, that the protection so purchased will be given when needed through the continued solvency of the issuing insurance carrier. These legitimate public interests cannot be protected in full measure without sound and effective rate regulation.[80]

---

period of experience used is too long or too short, or that too many cases are still in reserve, or that he thinks the trend factors are too steep or too flat, or that lawyers are about to become less zealous, or that the companies seem to be solvent enough, or what have you." Marryott, Franklin P., *op. cit.*, p. 37.

[78] See above, Note 2, Chapter I.

[79] Sawyer, Elmer W., *op. cit.*, p. 100.

[80] Memorandum by committee of American Mutual Alliance, 1946. Quoted in Marryott, Franklin J., "Mutual Insurance Under Rate Regulation," *Law and Contemporary Problems,* Vol. XV. No. 4 (Autumn 1950), p. 555.

Patterson said that protection of the public against financially unsound enterprises was "the chief *raison d'etre* of the insurance commissioner."[81] There continues to be accord among insurance authorities that promotion of the public welfare requires, above all else, prevention of insurer insolvency.[82] Unanimity is lacking, however, on the precise role of rates and rate regulation in this regard. To remain solvent a company must receive income sufficient to pay its losses and expenses. But sound investment policy, maintenance of adequate reserves, and efficient management also are essential. The use of adequate rates is therefore necessary, but not sufficient to prevent insurer insolvency, and there is disagreement on the extent to which action by regulatory authorities is necessary to prevent the companies from charging inadequate rates.

Another objective of rate regulation is equity or fairness in insurance pricing. Rates are not to be unfairly discriminatory nor are they to be excessive. These standards are subordinate to that of rate adequacy; "security is prized above premium savings."[83] When a crude rate is felt to be substantially safer than one based on a more highly refined and hence more equitable classification system, equity is normally sacrificed for rate adequacy.

It has been seen that concern with excessive rates was one of the factors motivating the establishment of insurance rate regulation. The antitrust approach to insurance regulation was abandoned early in the century, a move which received congressional sanction in 1945. But by electing to permit concerted action in insurance pricing, the states validated the type of activity through which, in the absence of public control, excessive and monopolistic rates could be secured by the industry. It was therefore incumbent upon the states to prevent exploitation of the legalized joint pricing. As expressed by the Merritt Committee, "not only is combination necessary for equitable rating, but conversely the making of equitable rates is the consideration which should be demanded of the companies for the right to combine."[84]

Another objective of rate regulation is the encouragement of

---

[81] Patterson, Edwin W., *op. cit.,* p. 192.

[82] See, e.g. Dineen, Robert E., *op. cit.,* p. 21.

[83] Otto, Ingolf H. E., "Regulation of Insurance in the United States by the Federal Government" (Unpublished Ph.D. dissertation, George Washington University, 1959), p. 10.

[84] *Insurance Hearings,* p. 2828.

competition. In submitting to the House of Representatives the bill which became the McCarran Act, the Committee on the Judiciary said, "It is the opinion of Congress that *competitive* rates on a sound financial basis are in the public interest."[85] The attainment of this objective is promoted partly through the requirement that rates be adequate. This standard is available to prevent the use of below-cost pricing as a means of forcing out competitors and achieving monopoly.

There is very considerable disagreement, however, on just how much price competition is desirable. In the view of some persons competition should be regarded as the prime regulator of insurance and few limitations should be placed upon it. The declared objective of the investigation of insurance by the Antitrust and Monopoly Subcommittee of the United States Senate, for example, is "to determine whether state laws and regulations have permitted competition to operate in the most effective manner consistent with the public interest."[86] Other leaders of industry and government reject the view that competition in itself is a primary objective, stressing instead the value of the stability and uniformity gained through "such restraints upon competition as are needed" to facilitate the attainment of company solvency and equitable pricing.[87] The difference is largely one of emphasis; there is general agreement that competition should be promoted.[88]

Thus, insurance rate regulation involves two conflicting methods of insurance pricing. A fundamental problem of public supervision is to achieve the proper balance between price diversity and price uniformity; between competitive pricing and cooperative pricing; between free enterprise and public control.

[85] Quoted in Williams, C. Arthur, *op. cit.,* p. 45. Emphasis supplied.
[86] *First Insurance Report,* p. iii–iv.
[87] Marryott, Franklin J., "Rate Regulation Revisited," p. 40.
[88] See statement of National Association of Insurance Commissioners, *Insurance Hearings,* p. 4884.

CHAPTER IV

CONTROL OF PRICE COMPETITION:
THE ISSUES

It has been seen that governmental supervision of casualty insurance as it has thus far evolved in the United States includes state regulation of rates made by companies either jointly or individually. The purpose of rate regulation is to assure the use of reasonable rates and the maintenance of competition. The statutes providing for rate regulation are vague and their objectives are contradictory. Each insurance commissioner must rely largely upon his own judgement in determining how best to encourage competition and at the same time preserve the desirable (but noncompetitive) features of cooperative rate making. He must "steer a middle course," Carlson says, "between the Scylla of an extreme flexibility which would make the operations of a rating organization meaningless, and the Charybdis of insistence upon a uniformity which would act in the direction of stifling competition."[1]

Others say that attempts to steer a middle course are futile, particularly in a market as dynamic as that for automobile insurance. From this viewpoint, the industry is bound to end up either on the rocks or in the whirlpool, and it would be better to make a choice between the two and then take steps to minimize the casualties.

The issues are not clear; many conflicting considerations are involved, some of which concern technical knowledge and information not easily acquired. Public interests clash with private interests, the latter including those who seek larger shares of an industry with $6 billion in income: stock companies, mutual companies, agency companies, direct writers, bureau companies, independent companies, brokers, agents, executives. It is not surprising

[1] Carlson, Thomas O., *op. cit.,* p. 21.

that rational analysis of the issues is rare; "the questions have become emotional, almost religious."[2] It also is not surprising that state
regulators have made differing judgements of the issues.

PRICE COMPETITION AND DIVERSITY VS.
PRICE COOPERATION AND UNIFORMITY

State control of price competition in automobile insurance can
be categorized into three different approaches. These are the restrictive approach of those states which permit little or no price competition, the permissive approach of other states where scarcely any
attempt is made to limit competition, and the All-Industry pattern
which normally falls somewhere between the two extremes.

The Restrictive Approach

Price competition in automobile insurance is either severely
restricted or completely suppressed in those states where rates are
made by a state agency or by a rating organization to which all
companies must belong. The rationale of this approach is that the
chance of incurring payable losses is basically the same for all insurers and can be evaluated most accurately through pooling the
experience data of all carriers. Furthermore, expenses do not differ
greatly among companies, particularly if uniform commission scales
are employed. It is claimed, therefore, that cooperative rating is most
reliable and is the only way to avoid unfair competition.[3]

Among the industry groups favoring this approach have been
the participating mutuals. "It is manifest that any legislation which
would require or tend to establish uniformity in rates would work
to the advantage, at least for the short run, of insurers who operate
on the mutual or participating basis. Through their dividends they
can, in effect, underquote any risk they deem desirable."[4]

A number of stock bureau companies have also advocated drastic
restrictions upon price competition. The president of Home Insurance Company, for instance, told the Senate investigating com-

[2] Otto, Ingolf H. E., "The British Insurance Scene," *Journal of Insurance*, Vol. XXVIII,
No. 1 (March 1961), p. 109.

[3] See Hobbs, Clarence W., *op. cit.*, pp. 359–60.

[4] Brook, Herbert C., *op. cit.*, p. 608. The mutuals' advantage is denied in Marryott,
Franklin, J., "Mutual Insurance Under Rate Regulation," pp. 553–4.

mittee that "if we could talk about utopia in this business, it might be a good idea if everybody belonged to a rating organization, and there was no escape hatch."[5]

The restrictive aproach has been adopted officially by the 5 states discussed below. Bills reflecting this philosophy have been considered in recent years in at least 9 other states.[6] Additionally, specific rulings of commissioners in states with All-Industry laws sometimes seem to reflect the restrictive spirit.

Complete Uniformity—Automobile insurance rates are made by state agencies in Massachusetts and Texas. In Massachusetts, state-made rates apply only to the minimum bodily injury liability coverage which must be carried on all registered vehicles. Rate variations are permitted on other automobile insurance.[7]

Rates for all automobile coverages in Texas are promulgated by the Board of Insurance. They must be charged by all companies. Deviations from the stated rates are not permitted, but participating policies may be issued.[8]

In North Carolina automobile rates are made by a rating bureau to which all companies providing the coverage must belong. Prior to September 1961 rate variations were permitted upon approval of a formal deviation from the bureau rate. Since that date, according to a newly adopted law, no deviations are permitted. As in Texas, participating policies may be issued.[9]

Standard Rates with Deviation Restricted—In Louisiana and Virginia relatively few deviations from the standard rate are permitted. Rates in Louisiana are prescribed by a state rating commission. There are no independent filings, but the law does permit companies to deviate from the state rate.[10]

The situation in Virginia is similar to that existing in North Carolina before September 1961. The law provides for uniform

---

[5] Testimony of Kenneth E. Black, *Insurance Hearings*, p. 1583. Mr. Black was referring specifically to the fire insurance business, in which this attitude is much more prevalent than in automobile insurance.

[6] *Insurance Hearings*, pp. 1230–1.

[7] *Ibid.*, p. 1225.

[8] *Regulation of Insurance in Texas* (Austin: Texas Research League, 1958), p. 48.

[9] *The National Underwriter*, June 23, 1961, p. 1.

[10] The deviation procedure is reported to be very cumbersome. *Insurance Hearings*, pp. 1306–7.

deviations from the rates promulgated by a bureau to which all insurers must belong.[11] In this state independent liability filings are authorized but "they are so proscribed administratively as to be of no practical value as a means of competing."[12] A stamping office or audit procedure is employed by these three states and by Texas to enforce company conformity with the approved rates.[13]

The Permissive Approach

The laws of several states reflect the philosophy that competition is the best regulator of insurance prices and that competition need not and should not be sacrificed in order to ensure the success of concerted rate making.

The permissive approach is naturally favored by non-bureau companies in whose opinion "the public interest is better served where the standards prescribed by the rating laws are treated as outer boundaries of a relatively broad area for the interplay of healthy competition and experimentation."[14] Nonrestrictive price regulation is also supported by some federal officials who hold that "the legislative history of the McCarran Act supports the view that Congress intended that competition would continue as the prime regulator of the insurance business."[15]

Definition of Rate Standards—The All-Industry laws, with regard to maximum and minimum rate levels, say simply that rates are to be neither "excessive" nor "inadequate"; the terms are not defined. The laws of a few states define these standards in such a way as to establish a rather broad zone of reasonableness.

The statutes of California and Missouri interpret rate excessiveness in the following manner:

> No rate shall be held to be excessive unless (1) such rate is unreasonably high for the insurance provided and (2) a reasonable degree of competition does not exist in the area with respect to the classification to which such rate is applicable.[16]

[11] *Ibid.*, p. 4871.

[12] Testimony of Vestal Lemmon, *Ibid.*, p. 1202.

[13] Marryott, Franklin J., "Present Systems of Governmental Supervision," p. 558.

[14] Testimony of Vestal Lemmon, *Insurance Hearings*, p. 1206.

[15] McHugh, Donald P., "Federal Investigation of Insurance." Address at Arizona Insurance Day, University of Arizona, February 27, 1960, p. 3. (Mimeographed.) Also see statement of Senator O'Mahoney quoted in Cowee, John W., and Center, Charles C., *op. cit.*, p. 71.

[16] Quoted in Carlson, Thomas O., *op. cit.*, p. 58. The remainder of this section on the permissive approach is drawn from this source.

Arizona, Montana, and Oklahoma define excessiveness in a similar way, while in South Carolina rates are too high only if the companies using them have made execessive profits during the previous 5 years.

Inadequate rates are described by the laws of California, Missouri, and Oklahoma in this manner:

> No rate shall be held to be inadequate unless (1) such rate is unreasonably low for the insurance provided and (2) the continued use of such rate endangers the solvency of the insurer using the same, or unless (3) such rate is unreasonably low for the insurance provided and the use of such rate by the insurer using same has, or if continued will have, the effect of destroying competition or creating a monopoly.[17]

Utah and Nebraska define inadequacy in a rather similar fashion. In the laws of Arizona, Minnesota, and Rhode Island rate adequacy is interpreted in terms of company profit and loss.

Filing Requirements—The All-Industry laws stipulate that before new rates can be used they must be filed, along with supporting information, with the state insurance department. Price competition is given added encouragement in those states where filings are not required.

In Montana only rating organizations must make rate filings, while in California and Missouri no filings are required. The Idaho law calls for rate filings only if the insurance commissioner finds that reasonable competition does not exist.[18]

The All-Industry Approach

The great majority of states adopted the All-Industry laws with little modification. In those states insurance companies are free to choose between filing their own rates, using those filed by a rating organization, or deviating from the bureau rates. In any case the rates must be filed with the insurance commissioner and are subject to disapproval based upon his interpretation of excessiveness and inadequacy.

There appears to be little doubt that rate regulation in the All-Industry states has grown more liberal during recent years. In 1957 a committee of the National Association of Insurance Commissioners found it necessary to denounce a statement presented to it

[17] *Ibid.*
[18] *Ibid.* Filings are not presently being required. *Insurance Hearings,* p. 1205.

"to the effect that an assurance had been given in the State of Washington and should be given by the members of NAIC generally that filings of requests for deviations would be viewed from a predetermined attitude of resistance or opposition."[19] Statements of this nature were not unusual at that time. In the same year the general manager of the Inland Marine Insurance Bureau expressed the belief that "there can be no reasonable doubt that the duty of supervision is to reconcile every independent filing and every deviation with the paramount vital filings of the rating organization."[20]

The concept that bureau filings are paramount is a carry-over from pre-McCarran Act days when the rating organizations and their companies actually were in a controlling position. Although this attitude continues to be held in some quarters, particularly in fire insurance,[21] it is now losing favor.[22] This is indicated by the "nine principles" adopted in December, 1960 by three major stock agency company groups[23] which seek to enable bureau companies "to act individually with respect to rates and forms whenever deemed necessary in order to keep pace with competitive change." The principles proposed included (1) eliminate "prior approval"[24] of rate filings by the insurance commissioner so that filed rates could be used immediately, (2) establish definitions of the statutory rate standards, (3) eliminate requirements for adherence to bureau filings by member companies, and (4) permit any company to subscribe for all or part of a bureau's services without appointing the bureau to make filings on its behalf.[25] While a cynic might suggest that the bureau companies which use the American agency system have been forced into this liberalized frame of mind by the

[19] National Association of Insurance Commissioners, *Proceedings*, 1958, p. 44.

[20] McHugh, Donald P., "Rate Regulation Revisited," p. 108.

[21] *Ibid.*, pp. 107–108.

[22] "Those who were among the most militant supporters of rigid rating laws a little more than a decade ago have now joined forces with the independents in a movement to loose the bonds that shackle initiative in rate making." Roger Kenney, "Senate Subcommittee Hearings Making Imprint Upon Insurance Business," *U. S. Investor*, March 27, 1961, p. 28.

[23] Association of Casualty and Surety Companies, Inland Marine Underwriters Association, and National Board of Fire Underwriters.

[24] Actually, the All-Industry laws contain no prior approval requirements, filed rates being deemed approved unless disapproved by the commissioner during the waiting period. In practice, however, many states have operated on a prior approval basis. This proposal would eliminate the disapproval period and substitute a provision that rates would automatically become effective upon the date of filing.

[25] Press release, Insurance Information Institute, December 12, 1960, pp. 3–4. (Mimeo.)

competition from the independent direct-writing companies, the fact remains that the former group does now favor less restrictive rate regulation.

The increasing number of deviations and independent filings indicates that insurance commissioners may also have a more permissive attitude toward price competition. The number of such filings rose from 989 in 1948 to 5,928 in 1958. Whether this reflects simply a greater number of requests for rate differences or the intentional adoption of a liberalized regulatory policy remains to be seen.

THE CASE FOR RESTRICTING PRICE COMPETITION

Although a great deal has been said and written about insurance rate regulation, little of the discussion has focused explicity upon the control of price competition. Much of the public debate which has taken place can however be put into such a context.

The issues are extremely complex; judgment of them requires the weighing of many considerations. Analysis will be facilitated by presenting separately the cases for (1) restricting and (2) permitting price competition, rather than by attempting specific evaluations of each of the many pertinent points. As an expository device, the two positions will therefore be stated and explained in affirmative terms. In subsequent chapters the problems of administering the adequacy and excessiveness standards will be analyzed in the context of the evidence opposing and supporting price competition.

Competition May Endanger Company Solvency

It was stated in the previous chapter that the primary objective of rate regulation is the prevention of company insolvency. In businesses other than insurance the attrition of inefficient, high-cost producers is regarded as salutory; occasional insolvencies are a small price to pay for assuring that the public will be served by the efficient enterprises which survive the competitive struggle. The consequences of company failure in this instance are borne largely by company stockholders and employees. The cost of an insurance company failure, however, extends to the purchasers of the product, and even beyond that to persons completely uninvolved except as

26 *Insurance Hearings,* p. 1659.

claimants and dependents. Insurance company failures therefore are not in the public interest and their avoidance is a major goal of state regulation.

Several unique characteristics of the insurance transaction point up the necessity of restricting price competition. In most other businesses the transaction is completed when the product is sold. But in the insurance business the buyer receives a contract calling for the performance of future services when and if certain contingencies occur. This means that the total costs of an insurance policy are not known at the time of the sale. They depend upon future events and can only be estimated on the basis of past experience. This increases the likelihood that intense, uncontrolled competition could develop into a price war in which insurers would cut prices below the level of adequacy.[27] It also should be noted that the typical insurance buyer is not able to judge the quality of his purchase in this respect, depending as it does upon the financial condition of the seller at some point in the future.

Advocates of the restrictive approach hold that historical evidence confirms the belief that insurance price competition will tend to degenerate into harmful price warfare. In the history of American insurance 1,073 property-casualty companies have been forced to retire because of financial difficulties.[28] It was mostly as protection against such self-destruction that fire insurance companies initiated joint rate making and attempted to enforce price uniformity.

> There has been nothing in the record or the experience of fire insurance associations to suggest any fallacy in the conviction that competition in rates and selling costs has no rightful place in the insurance business. On the contrary, those frequent periods in which control over rates and commissions has not been effective have served only as severe object lessons in the necessity for rigid maintenance of rules if the solvency of the companies was to be a fact rather than a dim hope.[29]

The record of price warfare and company failures[30] leads to the surers were permitted to charge any price they wished, the struggle

----

[27] The report of the Merritt Committee contrasted the insurance and grocery businesses, saying that the cost of insurance "does not stare the underwriter in the face in the same way that the buying price of sugar confronts the grocer." *Ibid.*, p. 2805.

[28] Letter from Mr. H. F. Swanson, Assistant Manager and Secretary, American Mutual Alliance, Chicago, Ill., April 14, 1961.

[29] Wandel, William H., *op. cit.*, p. 144.

[30] Specific examples include the failure of two California automobile insurers "resulting from grossly inadequate competitive premium rates." *A Study of the Necessity and Form*

conclusion that "unregulated competition has had a fair trial. Its record is one of failure."[31] From this viewpoint, if automobile inwould be won by those few large and powerful companies which are in a position to kill off their weaker competitors one by one. Concentrating upon a single coverage or territory at a time, the large countrywide companies would be able to cover their losses elsewhere while their smaller rivals were forced into bankruptcy.[32] The sole survivors of uncontrolled price competition would be the big companies; the ultimate victim would be the general public.

Joint Pricing Produces More Reliable Rates

Insurance rates are based upon the law of averages and upon the assumption that the future will, within reasonable limits, repeat the past. Other things equal, the broader the record of past performance, the greater will be the accuracy of predictions drawn from it.

In most instances an individual company does not have a sufficient volume of business to render its own experience a reliable guide for rate making. Even large companies whose total experience in a state is sufficient to judge over-all changes in rate levels may have inadequate statistics for setting rates on specific territories and classifications.[33] It is therefore necessary for companies to pool their loss and expense data and base their rates upon the combined experience of the group.

Although joint pricing of insurance necessarily restricts price competition, that is not its main purpose. It is simply an extension of the insurance principle of averaging the cost of many similar exposures; the averaging, in this case, is based on the experience of several insurers rather than a single one. Furthermore, joint rate making does not eliminate competition among the cooperating companies. Competition on matters other than price continues. As

of State Regulation of Insurance Rates (San Francisco: California Department of Insurance, 1945), p. 7.

"Shortly before 1909 rate wars in the surety field caused the failure or reorganization of six of the leading companies." Donovan, James B., *op. cit.*, p. 10.

"In 1929 . . . the third largest fire company in the United States went out of business because of insolvency, and it was the outstanding rate cutter of the day." Testimony of J. Victor Herd, *Insurance Hearings*, p. 1665.

[31] Marryott, Franklin J., "Why Regulate Insurance Rates?" p. 310.

[32] *Insurance Hearings*, pp. 1466 and 4414; *The National Underwriter*, May 5, 1961, p. 2.

[33] Reasony, John A., *op. cit.*, p. 224.

stated by the Merritt Committee, "the companies that form a tariff organization are in the most intense competition with each other, and what the combination chiefly does is prevent this competition from producing havoc with the rates."[34]

Unrestricted Competition Threatens Joint Pricing

Since insurance rates must be based on broad averages and since these averages can be obtained only through pooling arrangements, "the operation of insurance rate making bureaus must be preserved and protected against conditions which will destroy them."[35]

It has been seen that the intent of rate regulation in most of the states is to provide the conditions under which insurers may choose freely between bureau membership and independent price setting. The feeling is growing among proponents of the restrictive approach that "the All-Industry model was 'balanced' too far in the direction of unrestrainable competition and has not proved to be sufficient to bring about a pattern under which the rating bureaus can survive."[36] While the effort to permit independence of action by those insurers who do not care to conform may be a laudable one, the companies that accept cooperative rate making must have a reasonable amount of protection or they will be unable to resist competitive pressures and joint pricing may break down completely.[37]

If all companies, whose loss and expense record is better in some particular way than the average used by the bureau, establish their own rates, the public will be offered a whole series of rates, with the bureau companies' rates the highest.[38] Under these conditions, how many bureau companies "will continue to be willing to remain obligated to use bureau filings in the face of attrition from non-members, one having a competitive edge in one line, another in some other; this one having a rate advantage, another, an attractive form of coverage?"[39]

[34] *Insurance Hearings*, p. 2821.
[35] "Where's the Cheer in Chaos?" *Journal of American Insurance*, Vol. XXXVII (January 1961), p. 11.
[36] Marryott, Franklin J., "Rate Regulation Revisited," p. 44.
[37] *The National Underwriter*, November 13, 1959, p. 10.
[38] See memorandum of New York State Insurance Agents, *Insurance Hearings*, p. 2150.
[39] Marryott, Franklin J., "Mutual Insurance Under Rate Regulation," p. 562.

In automobile insurance, both the number of deviation and independent rate filings, and the share of the coverage written at such prices are increasing. The bureau companies cannot let themselves continue to be bound by their self-imposed price uniformity. "Cooperative rate making is threatened with disintegration."[40]

It may be that no middle ground between uniformity and diversity of automobile insurance pricing can be sustained. Freedom of independent pricing "can soundly endure only so long as not too many choose to exercise it."[41] Once uniformity or at least substantial control by the organization companies breaks down, competitive pressure impels the complete collapse of the cooperative arrangements essential to sound insurance pricing. "After that there will be real free and open competition without anything even resembling a scientific basis for rates, and there will be no alternative but for the State to take over, and fix one rate applicable to all companies."[42] To avoid such an occurrence, it is said, state regulation must restrict price competition in automobile insurance.

The Danger of Commission Wars

The Merritt Committee reported that open competition not only had driven rates too low, but also had driven agents' commissions too high.[43] The paradox of company expense being forced upward by competitive pressure even while the selling price is moving in the opposite direction is explained by the strategic position occupied by property-casualty agents. This is especially true under the American agency system and involves (1) the agents' control of their business produced through personal contact with the policy-holders, (2) the short-term nature of the policies, and (3) the ability of the agent to shift renewals from one company to another. The result is that the companies in effect are compelled to buy their business from agents.[44] In periods of intense, uncontrolled competition the price (commission) level is bid up by the insurance companies, diverting premium income from its proper use and diminishing the policy-holder's security.

[40] *Best's Insurance Reports (Fire and Casualty)* (New York: Alfred M. Best Co., 1960), p. ix. Also see Marryott, Franklin J., "Rate Regulation Revisited," pp. 29–31.
[41] Marryott, Franklin J., "Mutual Insurance Under Rate Regulation," p. 561.
[42] Barry, John R., Quoted in *Insurance Hearings*, p. 3425.
[43] *Insurance Hearings*, p. 2838.
[44] Wandel, William H., *op. cit.*, p. 11.

Price Competition May Encourage Quality Reduction

If there is free price competition and if coverage is sold primarily on the basis of price, those who hold this viewpoint feel that some companies may reduce the quality of the product in order to meet the price offered by rival insurers. For instance, insurance can be sold more cheaply in the short run if the company skimps on loss reserves. Another way of making price cuts tolerable is the adoption of a restrictive claim settlement policy. The latter can easily be accomplished when the size of the average claim is small, as with automobile physical damage coverage; claimants are frequently unwilling to incur the delay and expense necessary to secure a reasonable settlement of such claims.

Another result of excessive price competition in automobile insurance is the adoption of overly restrictive underwriting practices. In order to hold claim costs to a minimum, certain companies make every effort possible to insure only the very best risks.[45] The result is that such companies are able to lower their rates still more while those insurers which have refrained from adopting a restrictive underwriting policy find themselves writing a greater proportion of poor risks and must therefore either raise their rates or sustain underwriting losses. Unless the latter group of companies is willing to absorb increasing numbers of below-average insureds, the market for voluntary insurance of poor risks will dry up, assigned risk pools will grow and demands for governmental action will rise.[46] "There is no better way to invite the government, state or federal, to enter the business than to allow the super-selectivity of risks, engendered by a headlong dash of so-called 'free and open competition' to create a vacuum in the insurance market and leave unfulfilled a public need for adequate coverage."[47]

Restrictions Are Needed to Prevent Market "Creaming"

Rather than achieve a low rate by means of super-selective underwriting, a company may elect to reverse the procedure. It may (1) file a low rate which has not actually been warranted by its past experience, (2) use the competitive advantage to secure a large

[45] *The National Underwriter,* November 13, 1959, p. 26. Also see statement of F. Britton McConnell, Insurance Commissioner of California, *Insurance Hearings,* p. 1864.
[46] *The National Underwriter,* February 5, 1960, p. 22.
[47] Johnson, H. Clay, quoted in *The National Underwriter,* October 30, 1959. p. 36.

number of new risks, and then (3) ruthlessly weed out the poor risks by cancellation or refusal to renew, retaining only the best risks in order to (4) justify the low rate.[48] A simplified procedure previously cited[49] is simply (1) to cut the rate, (2) secure the business, and then (3) raise the rate. Use of this method was charged by the president of the Corroon and Reynolds Groups:

> In New York State, Allstate, writing automobile business, started out on the basis of participating policies. And then the department, in conjunction with Allstate, looking into the crystal ball I referred to, said, "We agree with you, you can write this business at 25 per cent of the rate of the stock companies, off the bureau rates." And so they said go ahead. So on the basis of the privilege, Allstate went out and developed a terrific volume of business. Now what do we find? What they saw in the crystal ball wasn't there. So Allstate has gotten, in the meantime, an increase of 12.5 per cent, and now they have gotten another one of 18.9.

> And now, I think their rates are about 9 per cent below the bureau rates. But they accumulated the business on the basis they could write at 25 per cent off. . . . They say, "We can do it better than the average, therefore, let us go ahead." But then if it turns out that they were wrong, they have gotten a great deal of competitive advantage, because they have sold on the other basis, they have got the customers and the clients.[50]

If some companies are able to take the cream of the market, others are left with the dregs. With their price advantage the former companies are able to prosper as more and better risks are written at lower and lower rates; meanwhile, the bureau companies must increase their rates in order to insure an increasingly poor selection of business.[51] Such is the inevitable result, it is said, if automobile insurers are not required to accept, but instead are permitted to take unfair advantage of the disciplined, cooperative action which is essential to the making of equitable premium rates.

Competition Produces Excessive Numbers of Rates and Forms

"The automobile insurance business is . . . a confusing, complex world in which a great many companies are doing so many things that it is impossible to keep track of them."[52] Much of the confusion

[48] See testimony of Morton V. V. White representing the National Association of Insurance Agents, *Insurance Hearings*, pp. 1753-4.
[49] See Chapter II, discussion of Unfair Competition.
[50] Testimony of Barry, John M., *Insurance Hearings*, p. 1400. Also see pp. 1781 and 4676. The allegation is denied by Allstate. See testimony of George H. Kline, *Ibid.*, p. 1245.
[51] See discussion of selective underwriting in Chapter II.
[52] *The National Underwriter*, June 10, 1960, p. 23.

stems from the increasing multitude of rates and forms used by the various companies. Commissioner Parker of North Carolina put the problem in the following words:

> We find old, conservative insurance companies, which in the past have been the backbone of the rating bureaus, withdrawing from the bureaus and filing independently. We find companies offering all kinds of gimmicks in their policy forms and rates, giving their policies eye-catching names and using all sorts of methods to try to attract the attention of the insurance buying public to their particular product. All of this at times seems to be done without any particular thought of the public good they may accomplish or the financial soundness of what they are offering.[53]

It was not always this way. From 1936 until recent years a standard automobile policy form was used by almost all companies and there was an easily identifiable, if not completely uniform, "standard rate." With the development of the intense competitive pressures which now prevail, both policy and price standardization have broken down.

Vigorous competition among companies exists with respect not only to the gross premium charge, but also on many of its components, including territories, classification plans, age groups, price-of-car groups and excess limits tables. The profusion of filings include "safe driver plans, single limit policies, economy policies and family policies, and so forth, being spawned at such a rapid rate that no one—not even the keenest underwriter—can possibly be certain as to just what effect they will have not only on the respective companies using such plans, but also upon that great number of smaller companies of limited resources and a large stake in automobile underwriting."[54]

This flood of filings has resulted partly from the policy recently adopted by several bureaus of making "agency filings" on behalf of member companies which wish to depart from the bureau pattern. The Mutual Insurance Rating Bureau is reported to have filed 60 or 70 special automobile plans for its members and subscribers.[55] The National Automobile Underwriters Association made 76 special agency type filings between May 1959 and May 1961.[56]

[53] *Ibid.*, November 24, 1961.
[54] Kenney, Roger, "Why Automobile Underwriting Problem Defies Easy and Early Solution," *U. S. Investor*, April 3, 1961, p. 38.
[55] *The National Underwriter*, December 30, 1960, p. 16.
[56] *The National Underwriter*, May 26, 1961, p. 59.

Initiation of merit-rated automobile insurance has caused a deluge of new and unique filings. The plans differ from one another with respect to size of the possible discounts and surcharges, length of the experience period, definition of chargeable accidents, coverages involved, policy form, method of securing the accident record and so forth. In January 1960 there were said to be 26 different merit-rating plans in one mid-western state[57] and 30 in California.[58] In Illinois the insurance commissioner reported that the Monday after the National Bureau merit-rating plan was approved, 60 additional plans were filed, each different from the others![59]

One of the attributes of an enterprise economy generally thought to be desirable is the freedom of consumers to choose among alternative products available at a range of prices. Theoretically the buyers will evaluate the alternatives rationally and select the best buys. In so doing, they will reject the products which are overpriced, of inferior quality, or which do not possess the characteristics desired. Through this process of free choice, the consumers are presumed to become sovereign; producers are forced by competitive pressure to adapt their product design and pricing policies to meet the consumers' wishes. Little or no public supervision is necessary, the business being in effect regulated by the consumers.

This rationale, however, relies upon the actions of reasonably informed buyers. And in an insurance market where even underwriters, agents and adjusters are confused,[60] how can the average consumer be expected to act intelligently? The fact is that he cannot, particularly when faced with an overwhelming number of choices. In order to determine the "best" automobile insurance purchase, the buyer would first of all have to be informed of the alternative prices, rating plans, classification systems, policy forms, company types and agency systems. He also should investigate company underwriting, claim, reserve and investment policies. Then he would have to weigh the advantages and disadvantages of each of these features and apply them to his own needs and ability to pay. Of course this procedure is not followed by the buyers of other

[57] Lasseigne, M. L., "A Fight for Survival," *The Casualty and Surety Journal*, Vol. XXI (January 1960), p. 19.
[58] Evans, Harold G., *op. cit.*, p. 23.
[59] *The National Underwriter*, December 23, 1960, p. 4.
[60] *The National Underwriter*, January 13, 1961, p. 30.

products any more than it is followed by insurance purchasers. But for several reasons, price and product proliferation are more serious problems in insurance than in other businesses.

First, *price comparisons* are more difficult to make. This is because of the great number of prices and because intelligent assessment of them requires that they be related to the many policy and company characteristics outlined above. A low price, for example, might be due to a restrictive claim settlement policy, while a high price might reflect inefficiency rather than superior quality.

Second, *quality comparisons in advance of purchase* are more difficult because of the complex and intangible nature of the insurance guarantee,[61] and because of the many factors which affect its quality. The latter include characteristics of future company status and performance which in most other instances are not related to the quality of the good or service purchased. Few people even attempt to make quality comparisons. Most buy what they feel is the least expensive policy or follow the recommendation of a friend or neighbor.[62] Economist John Ise remarked that "there is generally no knowledge or rationality at all in the purchase of . . . insurance."[63]

Third, *quality comparisons even after the purchase* of an automobile policy are more difficult than is the case with most other products. The performance of an automobile or the taste of a cigarette are subject to frequent scrutiny by the purchaser. By comparison, the policyholder only rarely is able to check the performance of his company and agent;[64] even the testimony of friends is of little value, as it is of necessity based upon biased impressions of the handling of only one or a few claims.

Enforcement of a reasonable degree of standardization in rates and policy forms would facilitate the analysis of alternative purchases by consumers. Advocates of a more restrictive regulatory policy say that this is necessary if the pressure of an informed consumer demand is to compel insurers to follow those practices which are in the public interest.

[61] See discussion of structure of the market in Chapter II.
[62] This was the finding of the 1956 National Bureau study cited above, Chapter II.
[63] Ise, John, *Economics* (New York: Harper, 1946), p. 167.
[64] Cf. Wallace, Donald H., "Industrial Markets and Public Policy," *Public Policy*, ed. Friedrich, C. J., and Mason, Edward S. (Cambridge: Harvard University Press, 1940), p. 112.

Greater standardization would also increase public confidence in the insurance business. Buyers would not have to fear restrictive policy phraseology, and they could be more confident that the premium rate was proper. For the companies, relative uniformity would secure the advantages of the joint pricing system, including its operating economies and reliable statistics.

Agents would also benefit from greater standardization. Their task would be enormously simplified if public regulation permitted only a limited number of deviations from well-known standard rates and forms.

Finally, regulation would be both facilitated and improved if the flood of independent and deviation filings were reduced. Prompt and adequate scrutiny of all rate and form revisions is now practically impossible,[65] particular in the many insurance departments forced to operate under severe budgetary restrictions. In Iowa, for example, one man is responsible for reviewing approximately 1,100 rate filings per month![66] The Ohio Superintendent of Insurance in 1959 spoke of "the impossible task state departments are saddled with in carrying out their duties of rate approval."[67] "Most of the departments," he said, "and Ohio is no exception, are so thoroughly ensconced in meeting the day-by-day deadlines and processing the hourly work load that little or no time can be given to imaginative or progressive original thinking."[68] By restricting price competition in automobile insurance, it is said, not only would the task of state regulation be facilitated, but its efforts would be supplemented by the pressure of an informed public opinion.

THE CASE FOR PERMITTING PRICE COMPETITION

The arguments for restricting price competition in automobile insurance, while accepted by many people, leave many others unconvinced. It is sometimes suggested by the latter group that the acceptance of joint rate making and the concept that bureau rates are paramount is due to the ability of rating bureaus to sell the type

[65] Marryott, Franklin J., *loc. cit.*

[66] *The National Underwriter*, May 26, 1961, p. 10.

[67] Vorys, Arthur I., "Insurance Supervision and Current Trends," *Insurance Counsel Journal*, Vol. XXVI (January 1959), p. 47.

[68] *Ibid.*, p. 43.

of regulation they prefer, rather than to any widespread public demand for protection against company insolvency.[69]

In sustaining an independent rate filing in 1957 the New York commissioner said:

> . . . the Insurance Law provides at the very beginning that the main purpose is "to promote the public welfare"; and secondarily and in aid of such purpose to provide cooperative action. There is nothing in the Law which says that the rating bureau shall be paramount. To hold otherwise would not be in the public interest. As a matter of fact, competition in the public interest is encouraged. What is meant by competition is that it shall be clean, open and reasonable. There is no mischief in that kind of competition. The laws which had for their purposes the modification of anti-monopoly pronouncements were justified with respect to rate making in the insurance field by the belief that the combination of experience would more readily lend itself to practical rates. But in permitting this combination through rating bureaus, it was not intended to destroy competition and to make rates uniform.[70]

Free Enterprise Ideals Are Appropriate to Insurance

The case for permitting price competition in automobile insurance basically rests upon the belief that the ideals of free enterprise are as applicable to insurance as to other businesses. This is the philosophy expressed by a former insurance commissioner of Michigan:

> If the doctrine of private enterprise is to endure in America, economic freedom must be preserved. . . . The Independents provide a factor of cardinal importance in the scheme of private enterprise. They provide competition. The competition they provide acts to prevent monopolistic control. By virtue of their existence, the balancing factor of consumer preference is given the freedom so essential to the operation of the doctrine of "Free Enterprise." The wisdom and virtue of the concept of Independents is basically the wisdom and virtue of the concept of Democracy in America.[71]

The ultimate goal of public regulation must be the welfare of the policyholders. Advocates of the permissive approach feel that regulation is necessary in order to assure that policyholders can

[69] Sawyer, Elmer W., "Can We Audit the Past in Terms of the Future?" *Insurance Law Journal*, May 1949, p. 364.

[70] Decision of New York Insurance Department, In the Matter of the Independent Rate Filing for Dwelling Classes by the North America Companies, September 4, 1957. Quoted in *Insurance Hearings*, p. 4901.

[71] Navarre, Joseph A., Quoted in Epes, W. Perry, "Rate Regulation Revisited," *Insurance and Government* (The University of Wisconsin Insurance Series, Vol. II, No. 4; Madison: Fund for Insurance Education and Research, 1960), p. 50.

secure sound coverage at proper prices. But they add that public control should not extend beyond this point to unnecessarily shelter the companies from competitive pressures. Rather, state supervisory officials should to the fullest extent possible shelter competition from efforts to restrict it by companies acting in concert. State regulators "must never assume that a private elite is capable of superintending the public interest."[72]

Concern over insurer solvency should not be permitted to pervert the regulatory goal of public protection into a doctrine of price uniformity.[73] When a single rate level is imposed upon all companies, such a concern will require that the rates be set at a level high enough to permit a profit by the high-cost companies.

Competitively determined rates, on the other hand, give the public the benefit of low-cost insurance protection. It is estimated that automobile coverage sold by members of the National Association of Independent Insurers results in savings to the public of $350 million annually.[74] This figure would be even larger were it not for the price uniformity imposed upon insurers in some states. Texas, for example, deprives its citizens of approximately $34 million each year by preventing the companies which would like to charge lower rates from doing so.[75]

Proponents of the permissive approach say that within the limits of flagrantly excessive or inadequate rates, insurers should be given freedom to experiment and progress. Regulators should resist the temptation to substitute their judgment for that of competent officials of sound companies.[76] A former New York commissioner expressed this point of view when he said: "I do not care if an Insurance Commissioner has the wisdom of Solomon, if he has the integrity of Abraham Lincoln, and if he has the research facilities of the General Motors Company—he cannot do as good a job in regulating rates as open competition can do."[77]

[72] McHugh, Donald P., *op. cit.*, p. 127.
[73] Testimony of Vestal Lemmon, *Insurance Hearings*, p. 1228.
[74] *Ibid.*, p. 1234 .
[75] *Ibid.*, p. 1196.
[76] Kline, George H., "Casualty Rates and Rating," *Insurance Counsel Journal*, Vol. XXVI (January 1959), pp. 51–2.
[77] Dineen, Robert E., "The Regulator's Viewpoint," *The Implications of Federal Control Over Insurance* (Insurance Series, No. 66; New York: American Management Association, 1946), p. 6.

Determination of a Proper Uniform Rate
Is Neither Feasible Nor Justifiable

The dilemma faced by insurance regulators who seek to reconcile different rate filings was mentioned in Chapter I. In the example given there of $50 and $70 filings, the problem was whether to approve one or the other or both, or to insist upon a compromise which might very well constitute an inadequate rate for one of the companies and an excessive rate for the other.

The differences in the rate filings of various companies may be due to any number of factors. Sometimes they reflect the use of different loss statistics. Even if companies pool experience data, resulting in common pure premiums, an allowance for profit and expense must be added. The amount necessary to cover these factors will vary among companies depending upon company size, type, efficiency, commission scale, advertising budget and so forth.

Furthermore, it should be remembered that insurance rate making is "not an inevitably accurate and scientific calculation."[78] It requires personal interpretation and judgment[79] at its every step. Therefore, not only is a rate which is proper for one company not necessarily so for another, but what appears to be a proper rate in the estimation of one person is not necessarily proper in the judgment of another.[80] From this viewpoint there can be more than one reasoned and reasonable judgment as to the proper level of rates; there is no basis for presuming that the judgment of the insurance commissioner or of a rating bureau is superior to that of an independent filer. "Large portions of bureau filings have little more than informed judgment to support them. Why, then, should not informed judgment of financially sound, competently managed individual companies be given credence?"[81]

Those who would impose drastic restrictions upon price competition in this field apparently assume that the automobile insurance

[78] Carlson, Thomas O., "Statistics for the Ratemaker," *Proceedings of the Casualty Actuarial Society,* Vol. XL, No. 3 (May 1953), p. 1.

[79] The laws of six states specifically include "judgment" as one of the bases of rates. Carlson, Thomas O., "Rate Regulation and the Casualty Actuary," pp. 59–60. The All-Industry laws list a number of items to be considered in rate making, including "all other relevant factors." Sec. 3 (a).

[80] Smith, Bradford, Jr., "Current Developments in Insurance Rate Regulation," *Insurance Law Journal,* No. 445 (February 1960), p. 80.

[81] Testimony of Vestal Lemmon, *Insurance Hearings,* p. 1216.

industry is comparable to the public utilities whose rates are fixed by regulatory commissions.

In most public utilities, economies of scale are pronounced, demand fluctuates widely, and duplication of facilities is wasteful or unworkable. The firms are under pressure to spread their high fixed costs over as great a volume of business as possible. As a result, it is not unlikely that competition would push rates so low that most of the competitors, if there were any, would be driven out of business. For these and other reasons,[82] price competition is regarded as impractical, and the industries are given exclusive franchises by the government. In return for this sole right to supply service in the area, the government reserves the right to regulate the business in order to prevent abuse of the monopoly power it has granted.

Automobile insurers are not public utilities. They are not granted government franchises; they are not monopolies; they are not required to make their services available to all who request it; they do not have large fixed costs and economies of scale; they do not face a widely fluctuating demand; and there are no physical conditions which would justify limiting entry of qualified companies into the field.[83] Therefore the justifications of price uniformity which exist in the field of public utilities are totally absent in automobile insurance.

Price Warfare Causing Insolvencies Is Now Highly Unlikely

It has been remarked that much of what is said about the whole question of property-casualty rate making in the United States represents superstition or tradition rather than factual knowledge.[84] In the opinion of those who favor price competition, this is probably nowhere more true than in the discussion of the rate wars which, it is alleged, have resulted in the past and would occur again if price competition is not rigidly controlled.

The terms "price warfare" and "cut-throat competition" are seldom defined by those who use them. In many cases, the party

[82] See Troxel, Emery, *Economics of Public Utilities* (New York: Rinehart Co., 1947), pp. 3–48.

[83] National Association of Insurance Commissioners, *Proceedings*, 1952, pp. 590–1.

[84] Testimony of Otto, Ingolf H. B., *Insurance Hearings*, p. 1052.

complaining of such conditions is simply finding it more difficult to achieve the same profit rate enjoyed in palmier days before competitors made their presence felt.[85]

No thorough study of insolvencies in the property-casualty insurance business has ever been made.[86] It is certain, however, that there have been no rate wars since adoption of the All-Industry laws,[87] and it is doubtful that there ever was a sustained, widespread rate war which, in itself, caused the failure of many previously sound insurers.[88]

One of the primary objectives of company managers, after all, is to conduct a financially successful enterprise. There is no reason to expect that insurers would like to become involved in price warfare, and it has been seen that economic conditions in the industry are not those of "natural monopoly." Even if a giant company precipitated a rate war and drove its rivals out of business, it could not perpetuate its advantage. As soon as it raised its rates to the level necessary to cover total costs, new competitors would be attracted by the freedom of entry, low fixed costs and profit possibilities of the business.

The Merritt Committee—Those who equate rate competition with chaos find much of their inspiration in the 1911 report of the Merritt Committee. The report, as described above,[89] stated that open competition led to rate cutting and called for state regulation of rates. But it is improper to conclude, as is sometimes done,[90] that the Merritt Committee proved that insurance competition is likely to degenerate into destructive competition which will cause both the industry and the public to suffer.

[85] Sawyer, Elmer W., *loc. cit.*; Brook, Herbert C., *op. cit.*, p. 620.

[86] Heins, Richard M., "Liquidations of Insurance Companies," *Insurance and Government* (The University of Wisconsin Insurance Series, Vol. II, No. 3; Madison: Fund for Insurance Education and Research, 1960), p. 54.

[87] Statement of Alfred J. Bohlinger, *Insurance Hearings*, p. 1794.

[88] In his three-volume work, A. F. Dean devotes considerable attention to the chaotic conditions faced by local agents and the price discrimination among individual risks which prevailed during the anti-compact period. But with regard to the effect of rate warfare upon company solvency, he says: "Where a rate war extends to an entire state, it may determine the retirement of a weak company or two at the end of the year, but as a whole, it simply serves to increase the average cost ratio of the country by a small percentage." Dean, A. F., *The Philosophy of Fire Insurance*, Vol. I (Chicago: Edward B. Hatch, 1925), p. 78.

[89] See Chapter III.

[90] *E.g.*, Backman, Jules, *op. cit.*, p. 99.

Considerable doubt can be cast upon some of the conclusions drawn in that Report in view of the paucity of factual findings to support the conclusions. But whatever its virtues or defects, the Report is significant only as a historical document reflecting a state of the industry fifty years ago, with recommendations appropriate to the times. To cite this document in 1960 as infallible gospel, as do the insurance traditionalists dedicated to their belief in "stability" as the economic millenium, is to ignore what has been occurring in the market place during the last several decades.[91]

The report contains no documentation whatever of its assertation that unrestricted price competition had led to company insolvencies. While no proof that this had not happened is available either, a review of the literature leads one to feel, like Carlson, that the results of the failure of competition as a regulative force "were not nearly as vicious as many people would have us believe."[92]

Equally important has been the tendancy to interpret the Merritt Committee report in the context of present day conditions and to ignore the changes in rate making and regulation which have occurred in the past half-century.

The report mentioned the procedure which had recently been inaugurated in life insurance whereby the companies were combining their experience under the auspices of the Actuarial Society of America. It went on to say:

> This is very different from anything that has been done with the corresponding problem in fire insurance. Strange as it may seem, rating organizations in the fire insurance business do not themselves possess any classified experience. The companies to be sure keep their classifications, but these figures are not combined and the rating is done by a committee which makes the rates upon the basis of a comparison of the members' own underwriting experience. Attempts frequently have been made by underwriters to induce the companies to combine their experience as a basis for use in making rates, but these attempts have invariably failed. The reason for this is that a company considers its experience a trade secret and is so jealous of it that it will not submit to its being used for the public good.[93]

Viewing these conditions in 1911, one might well be led to believe that there was a strong case for mandatory company membership in a rating organization which would pool the experience of all companies and set rates subject to governmental approval. Today,

---

[91] McHugh, Donald P., *op. cit.*, p. 98.
[92] Carlson, Thomas O., "Rate Regulation and the Casualty Actuary," p. 49.
[93] *Insurance Hearings*, p. 2824.

however, company experience data are no longer considered to be a trade secret. Insurance companies are now aware of the need for a broad rate base and will pool their statistics voluntarily if they feel it is desirable. Mandatory bureau membership and rate uniformity are no longer prerequisite to sound rate making.

A fact often overlooked, however, is that even the Merritt Committee did not recommend the elimination of price competition. The most frequently quoted portions of the report are those which explain the need for a broad statistical basis for rates and those which criticize the results of "open competition." Seldom cited is the section headed THE REGULATION OF RATES BY COMPETITION. After noting that competition among conference companies in rates and commissions had been eliminated by combination, and that competition in policy forms had been closed by policy standardization, this section of the report states:

> It has been urged, however, in this report, that competition, with the help of publicity, was sufficient to keep rates reasonable. If this is so, competition must still have some power. *It is true to be sure that perfectly free competition in rates has been largely closed, and it is believed that this is unquestionably for the public good, but competition can and does regulate rates through the medium of the rating organizations.*
>
> If a rate is too high there is pressure brought by companies upon the rating organization to reduce the rate as a basis for securing business, that is, there is a competition among the companies to obtain the favor of the insured by securing for him a reduction in rate. Furthermore, there is the competition of mutual and non-Board companies and the threatened competition of other companies that will be organized if the rate becomes too high.[94].

The following section, on mutual insurance, says that "this beneficial and regulative form of competition should be retained and increased if possible."[95]

The point is that in explaining the advantages of cooperative rate making, the Merritt Committee was not urging the elimination of all price competition. It must be remembered that this was a period of considerable antitrust fervor; one of the purposes for which the committee was created by the New York Legislature was to investigate the advisability of adopting an anti-compact law like

[94] *Ibid.*, p. 2847. Emphasis in original.
[95] *Ibid.*

those which recently had been put into effect by a number of other states.[96] The Committee opposed anti-compact legislation; that is it opposed mandatory competition (the antitrust approach). In doing so, it took great pains to demonstrate that insurance rating organizations were not "trusts" and that the unique characteristics of the insurance business made concerted pricing beneficial and, to some extent, essential. The committee report recommended that co-operative pricing not be banned, but that it be legalized and regu-lated. On the assumption that this would be done, *the Merritt Committee did not oppose, and in fact favored, price competition.*

Commission Wars Now Unlikely—A recurrence of the commis-sion wars which the Merritt Committee found 50 years ago is highly improbable, it is claimed, if insurers continue to be able to compete on the basis of price. Former commission wars took place in an environment where price uniformity generally prevailed. Except when enforcement of the single price system broke down and rate wars developed, the major competitive weapon was the commission scale. But if insurers are free to deviate from the standard rate level and to offer alternative policy forms and rating systems, there is little incentive to increase the price paid to the company agents.

As long as the traditional agency system is faced with vigorous rivalry from the direct writers, commission wars in automobile insurance are almost inconceivable. In fact, American agency sys-tem companies in recent years have lowered their commission rates in order to make their product more competitive. This has demon-strated the validity of Hensley's statements that "competition in commissions can be overcome . . . by strong enough price competi-tion from other types of insurers, or other methods of selling, to make the sale of the product through higher commissions and resultant higher premiums quite difficult."[97]

Absence of Regulation Elsewhere—The simplest refutation of the case for strict rate regulation, say its opponents, is the fact that in England and for certain major classes of insurance in the United States there is no supervision of rates. In spite of this, the dire pre-

[96] *Ibid.*, p. 2793.
[97] Hensley, Ray J., *op. cit.*, p. 40.

dictions of those who claim that rigid public control is essential have not come true in these instances.

The general philosophy in England has been that the government should have only limited supervisory powers over the insurance business.[98] Neither rates not policy forms must be filed or approved[99] and there are no statutory stipulations concerning rate reasonableness or joint pricing.[100]

Regulation of English insurance is supplied primarily by the industry itself, particularly through the Accident Offices' Association, a stock insurer rating organization. The member companies (tariff companies) write the bulk of the automobile insurance business, in competition with Lloyds and a numbers of nontariff companies. Both of the latter groups are, of course, free to devise their own rates and forms. But although rate wars are possible, they have been rare.[101] Rather, the companies have benefitted from the ability to charge whatever rates are appropriate without having to justify them to government officials.[102] "The reputation of British insurance companies for financial strength is excellent in England and throughout the world."[103]

In the United States there is little or no regulation of the rates charged by life, marine, or commercial health insurers. The lack of public supervision over life insurance rates is sometimes justified by pointing out that reserve requirements assure their adequacy, while competition prevents the establishment of excessive rates.[104] Furthermore, the life insurance business is very stable and is little subject to catastrophe. Determination of rates is almost purely a mathematical process;[105] the life insurance business "has automatic

[98] Those companies which are not exempt from supervision are regulated by the Board of Trade, the Insurance Section of which had a staff of about ten persons in 1948. Bohlinger, Alfred J., and Morrill, Thomas C., *Insurance Supervision and Practices in England* (New York: State of New York Insurance Department, 1948), p. 10.

[99] *Ibid.*, pp. 19–20.

[100] *Ibid.*, p. 25.

[101] *Ibid.*, p. 39. The authors felt that this was "probably because of the underlying conservatism of British methods of doing business." This was apparently one of the major reasons why they recommended that New York adopt rate regulatory legislation instead of attempting to follow the British pattern.

[102] *Ibid.*, p. 73.

[103] *Ibid.*

[104] Mehr, Robert I., and Osler, Robert W., *Modern Life Insurance* (New York: Macmillan Co., 1956), p. 692.

[105] Dineen, Robert E., Procter, Clifford R., and Gardner, H. Daniel, *op. cit.*, p. 22.

rate regulation built into a mortality table, a reserve table and an interest factor."[106]

> But when marine and accident and health are brought in as further examples of workable competition in rates, these answers do not apply: Marine and accident and health insurance are two of the least stable, least mathematical, and most subject to judgment lines in all of insurance. And it is instructive to note that while we hear many complaints about practices and behavior in accident and health insurance business, these complaints do not include the charge that the companies in this branch of the business are not making enough money or that they are competing each other into the poorhouse.[107]

How, then, have marine and health insurers avoided ruinous price competition? They have done so by exercising their own good judgment.[108] There is no reason to believe that automobile insurers would not demonstrate similar judgment if they were freed from the restraint of public control.

Assertions that uncontrolled price competition will cause insolvencies and public harm are thus said to be refuted by experience in other places and other lines of insurance as well as by the lessons of history and economics.

Rate Regulation Cannot Prevent Company Failures

It has been seen that the main objective of rate regulation is to prevent the use of inadequate rates which would lead to company insolvency. It is, of course, true that the rates charged and premiums received must be sufficient to cover loss payments and company expenses. And it is also true that a number of insurers become insolvent each year. But it does not necessarily follow that the cause of these companies' financial difficulties was the charging of inadequate rates.

Statistics on the number of failures which have resulted in loss to stockholders or to claimants are not available. The great majority of the companies which retire from business apparently either merge or reinsure their policy obligations with other insurers so that little or no loss is sustained by the owners or the general public.

The American Mutual Insurance Alliance reports that out of

---

[106] *The National Underwriter*, May 5, 1961, p. 24.
[107] Statement of Bob A. Hedges, *Insurance Hearings*, p. 1111.
[108] *Ibid.*

5,678 property-casualty retirements in the history of the United States, 1,073 or 18.9 per cent of the companies were forced to retire because of financial difficulties.[109] There is no information available to show the proportion of these companies which were unable to liquidate their claims. Even more pertinent, there is no way to determine how many, if any, of these failures were caused by the use of inadequate rates.

In the absence of empirical data on the cause of insurance company insolvencies, one must turn to the testimony of experienced insurance officials. In the opinion of many of these men, all or almost all insolvencies have been due to factors other than rate inadequacy. The following statement is typical:

> If any affirmative case has ever been made that insurance failures result from inadequate rates or from rate competition, it has been kept hidden from public knowledge. All the evidence runs in the opposite direction.
>
> Failures are the result of management excesses and incompetence. It is not the adequacy of the rate, but the failure of management to live within the rate which causes underwriting disasters. Even then, *it is difficult to trace any important failure in modern times to rate inadequacy per se.* In order of importance, failures are due to (1) inadequate initial financing, (2) poor underwriting, including the assuming of uninsurable hazards, (3) excessive operating expenses, including commissions, and (4) poor investments.[110]

The Special Counsel of the Liquidation Bureau of the New York Insurance Department has compiled a list of the irregularities leading to liquidation proceedings in that state during the past 30 years.

[109] Swanson letter, *loc. cit.*

[110] Morrill, Thomas C., "Discussion on the Economics and Principles of Insurance Supervision," *Insurance and Government* (The University of Wisconsin Insurance Series, Vol. II, No. 1; Madison: Fund for Insurance Education and Research, 1960), p. 88. Emphasis Supplied. Mr. Morrill is Vice President of State Farm and former Deputy Superintendent of Insurance of New York.

For similar statements see testimony of: Vestal Lemmon, General Manager of National Association of Independent Insurers, *Insurance Hearings,* p. 1229; Henry C. Moser, Senior Vice President of Allstate, *Ibid.,* p. 1250; Alfred J. Bohlinger, former Insurance Superintendent of New York, *Ibid.,* p. 1794; F. Britton McConnell, Insurance Commissioner of California, *Ibid.,* p. 1886.

Also see Brook, Herbert C., *op. cit.,* p. 622; McHugh, Donald P., "The Challenge to State Regulation of Insurance," Address before South Carolina Insurance Forum, February 1, 1961, p. 10 (Mimeographed); Albert H. Mowbray, *Insurance, Its Theory and Practice in the United States* (3rd ed.; New York: McGraw-Hill, 1946), p. 458.

Also see Archie Nichols, "The Liquidation of Insurance Carriers in the Commonwealth of Pennsylvania," *The Journal of Insurance,* Vol. XXVIII, No. 2 (June 1961). Nichols states that "if dishonesty could be regulated along with incompetency, failures could and would disappear." *Ibid.,* p. 49.

The list includes 22 different practices ranging from improper or dishonest underwriting, accounting, investment and claims procedures to "ineffective procedure for recovery of salvage arising from losses paid." The list does not include the charging of inadequate rates.[111]

Research conducted at the University of Wisconsin by Professor Richard M. Heins is reported to confirm the finding that rate inadequacy has not caused company failures. Professor Heins states that there have been two main causes of insolvency, management malfeasance and management inadequacy. He adds that there have been relatively fewer insolvencies in states having greater freedom in making rate filings than in those states with a restrictive regulatory policy.[112]

It appears, therefore, that inadequate rates are not the cause, and rate regulation cannot be the cure, of insurance failures. In other words, the theory that rate regulation is imperative for the maintenance of company solvency presupposes incompetence in the setting of rates, but still better opportunities for incompetent and destructive management exist in other aspects of company operation.[113] Even if full manual rates are charged, a company can easily become insolvent through poor risk selection or by inadequate control of expenses.

The fact that elimination of price competition does not eliminate the insolvency problem is demonstrated by the record of Texas, where rate uniformity is enforced by law. A total of 79 United States companies subject to rate regulation became insolvent during the period January 1, 1946 to May 15, 1959. Of these, 26, or almost one-third, were Texas companies. In contrast, California and Missouri, neither of which regulates rates at all, each had only 3 insolvencies.[114]

Rate control cannot achieve its major objective because what is an adequate rate for one company is often an inadequate rate for another. Even under a single-price system some companies will

[111] Bennett, Alfred C., "Liquidations of Insurance Companies," *Insurance and Government* (The University of Wisconsin Insurance Series, Vol. II, No. 3; Madison: Fund for Insurance Education and Research, 1960), pp. 31–2.

[112] *The National Underwriter*, November 24, 1961, pp. 7 and 26.

[113] Sawyer, Elmer W., *op. cit.*, p. 364.

[114] Data supplied by Vestal Lemmon, National Association of Independent Insurers.

prosper while others fail.[115] If price flexibility is permitted, the public will benefit by the companies' ability to adjust their rate levels in accordance with their own needs. If the government is to seek to promote insurer solvency, "the need is for regulation which aims at the demonstrated causes of financial disaster, and not at hypothetical causes."[116]

Restricting Price Competition also Limits Nonprice Competition

Another point made by the advocates of liberalized rate regulation is that although rigid controls may intend to limit only price competition, a necessary side effect is the restriction of other forms of competition. This is true because in order to effectuate a single price system, the same rate must be charged by all sellers *for the same product.* There can be no alteration in policy coverages or rating systems unless the change is instituted by all companies simultaneously. Since this deprives any individual company of the competitive advantage gained through research and innovation, changes simply do not take place until, and unless, they are forced upon all of the companies.

The ability to innovate is particularly important to small and new companies. The larger and older insurers ordinarily have an advantage in reputation, financial strength, and agency plant. Unless restrained by the regulatory system, the small company may be able to develop new and more efficient methods of operation or coverage, or it may concentrate upon a particular segment of the market where its ingenuity and flexibility give it an advantage over its larger rivals. Under a system of rigid public control, however, the small company may be forced to compete on the basis of high commission and dividend scales which keep it in a perpetually shaky financial condition and prevent it from supplying its potential in service to the public.[117]

The experience in Texas again illustrates the point. "Investigation fails to reveal a single instance in which a rating or coverage

---

[115] Underwriting experience of the 100 largest casualty companies for the 10-year period 1948–57 ranged from a profit of $81 million to a loss of $30 million. At each extreme was a company using bureau rates. *The Spectator,* Vol. CLXVII (March 1959), p. 30.

[116] Morrill, Thomas C., *loc. cit.*

[117] *The National Underwriter,* November 4, 1960, p. 36.

advance originated in the state of Texas."[118] Most of such changes have been pioneered by independent companies in other states and have not been adopted in Texas until several years later.[119]

Resistance to change has also been evident in many of the states having All-Industry laws. This has been attributed to cumbersome procedures of the rating bureaus[120] and to the insistence by insurance departments that filings for new plans and forms be accompanied by statistical justification even when there is no pre-existent experience.[121]

Opposition to change has been strongest in fire insurance[122] where the single policy philosophy is more deeply entrenched. To a lesser extent, it is corollary to any system under which price competition is artificially restricted. Only by permitting relatively free competition in the market-place can new ideas be easily and effectively tested, and outmoded concepts exposed and discarded.

Administrative Problems of Strict Public Control

Efforts to curtail price competition in automobile insurance raise several problems at the state administrative level which it is claimed would be less troublesome if competition were permitted.

Problems of Budget and Staff—The Senate Subcommittee reported that many of the insurance departments are under-staffed and that many pay inadequate salaries.[123] In 1957, the states spent $17 million on insurance supervision. This was only 4.27 per cent of the $456 million they collected in premium taxes on a total of over $25 billion in premium volume.[124] Apparently many of the insurance departments are primarily tax collecting agencies.

While states like New York and Illinois evidently have adequate staffs, insurance departments in other states obviously have "neither the budget, the manpower nor the necessary competence"[125] to

118 *Ibid.*, September 9, 1960, p. 4.
119 *Ibid.*
120 Brook, Herbert C., *op. cit.*, p. 615.
121 *Insurance Hearings*, p. 4692.
122 "Traditional habits of thought which had persevered for many years had encrusted this branch of the industry with attitudes stultifying progress and hostile to new ideas." McHugh, Donald P., "Rate Regulation Revisited," p. 100.
123 *First Insurance Report*, p. 136.
124 *Ibid.*, p. 151.
125 U. S. Senator Estes Kefauver, Press release, January 23, 1961, p. 4, (Mimeographed.)

carry out their responsibilities effectively. Utah, for instance, had one man in 1957 to check the annual reports of almost 600 companies in three weeks' time,[126] and there was not a single person "equipped by training and experience critically to scrutinize filed rates and supporting statistics."[127] As a result, the department relied heavily upon bureau filings, generally accepting them without question and using them as a standard for judging non-bureau filings, "except when pressures are sufficiently concentrated to be felt through the political mechanism."[128]

Other examples include South Carolina, where the Insurance Commissioner recently appealed for more funds, stating that the department lacked sufficient manpower to check the 3,000 policy forms filed with it each week.[129] And in Wisconsin, it is reported, inadequate staffing caused the department to approve automobile rate increases in 1948 and 1951 without even checking the filed statistics.[130]

The Senate Investigating Committee obtained information concerning the quantity of materials which were processed by 45 states during a three-month period in 1959. The materials included rate filings and rating plans, policy forms and endorsements, underwriting rules, and statistical plans. It was found that the average number of items processed per person engaged in rate supervision was 385. New York State processed 158 items per man. But in 21 states the workload was over 1,000 items per man for the period, and in 3 states, each person handled in excess of 7,000 items. The committee reached the obvious conclusion that in some states either the staffs were greatly overworked or that it was impossible for them to do a complete and effective rate supervisory job on this great volume of material.[131]

Increased appropriations would, of course, alleviate these problems, but the fault lies partly with the present regulatory system. To

[131] *Second Insurance Report*, pp. 90–93.

[126] Kimball, Spencer L., and Hansen, W. Eugene, "The Utah Insurance Commissioner: A Study of Administrative Regulation in Action," *Utah Law Review*, Vol. V, No. 4, (Fall 1957), p. 453.

[127] Kimball, Spencer L., and Boyce, Ronald N., *op. cit.*, p. 663.

[128] *Ibid*.

[129] The Commissioner added a request for replacement of the department's single adding machine, which had been purchased in 1921. *The National Underwriter*, November 11, 1960, p. 4.

[130] Kimball, Spencer L., *op. cit.*, p. 108.

appraise critically each of the thousands of filings received from hundreds of companies on many different kinds of insurance is an almost superhuman task. The states which attempt to cope with the situation become immersed in a quagmire of detail which, as Mr. Vorys said, leaves little or no time for original thinking and attention to matters of general department policy.[132] A number of persons have expressed the belief that much of this regulatory activity is not only ineffective but is also unnecessary and, to an increased extent, could be fulfilled more efficiently by the free play of competitive forces.[133]

Diversity of Regulatory Policies—A further problem concerns the diversity of regulation among the various states. Marryott has pointed out that if competition is permitted to force rates to low levels in certain states, other states which believe in more strict regulation may not long be able to continue a policy of requiring that more adequate rates be collected of their own citizens.[134] In more general terms, the same sort of Gresham's Law may prevail whenever there is a continuing interstate diversity in regulatory policy, whether the blame is put upon the states with high or low rates and strict or loose supervision. If, for example, automobile underwriting losses are sustained in New York State because its commissioner disapproves filings for rate increases, the companies may attempt to recoup their New York losses in states where the control is less strict. In any case, diversity in public controls has the effect of discriminating in favor of the policyholders of some states at the expense of those in other states. A general relaxation of the control of price competition would reduce this diversity and discrimination.

Political Influence—A final problem which is intensified by stringent control of price competition is that of political pressure upon the regulatory authorities. While the effects of such pressure cannot be proven, the many complaints of political influence indicate that it does exist and is a serious problem.[135]

[132] See above, Note 68.
[133] See *e.g.,* McHugh, Donald P., *op. cit.,* p. 125.
[134] Marryott, Franklin J., "Rate Regulation Revisited," pp. 38–40.
[135] Donovan, E. G., "Rate Regulation Revisited," p. 25; Kefauver, *op. cit.,* p. 3; Kimball, *op cit.,* pp. 107 and 313; Morrill, *op. cit.,* p. 89; Whitney, Simon N., *Antitrust Policies,* Vol. II (New York: Twentieth Century Fund, 1958), p. 353.

The Executive Vice President of the Royal Globe Insurance Companies said: "We regard political interference with rates as the greatest present-day threat to our business."[136] He added that the problem was most serious in automobile insurance.

The executive Vice President of the Insurance Company of North America explained the situation in this manner:

> All is well when the Commissioner is happily able to announce a *reduction* in insurance rates; but when it is necessary to *increase* them, he finds himself in a most unenviable position.
>
> However justified increases might be, it is felt to be the course of political "wisdom" to refuse them. This creates an impossible position for the business. We cannot make reasonable and adequate rates for insurance on a political basis. How much less costly it would be for the public if Commissioners were relieved of the burdensome responsibility of having to investigate and approve rates. How much better it would be for the companies to make and use the rates they need, taking the blame for increasing rates where necessary.[137]

If insurance companies feel they are wronged by the decisions of state rate regulators they can seek remedy by way of judicial review. This, however, has not proved to be satisfactory in meeting the needs of the volatile and competitive automobile industry.[138] Appeals to the courts are seldom successful even if the weight of the evidence seems to favor the filing company. The courts generally refuse to substitute their judgment for that of the insurance commissioner as long as some degree of plausibility attaches to his decision.[139]

Because such a large element of judgment is involved in both the construction and the evaluation of automobile rates, the commissioner can, in effect, take control of the rate making function. Coupled with the effects of political influence, the result is that the industry is forced to suffer from "a sort of administrative absolutism which, under present conditions, is intolerable."[140] This problem would, for the most part, be eliminated if insurers were free to establish their own rates within broad limits of reasonableness.

[136] Johnson, H. Clay. Quoted in Kenney, Roger, *loc. cit.*

[137] Smith, Bradford, Jr., *op. cit.,* p. 82.

[138] Donovan, James B., "State Regulation of Insurance," *Insurance Law Journal,* No. 396 (January 1956), p. 14.

[139] Marryott, Franklin J., *op. cit.,* p. 33.

[140] *Ibid.,* p. 34.

SUMMARY

These, then, are the arguments supporting and opposing a policy of strict public control over price competition in automobile insurance. Complete reconciliation of the two viewpoints is obviously impossible. They rest upon different values and upon different judgments as to what the results would be if the present regulatory pattern were changed.

Specifically, the two viewpoints contradict each other on the most fundamental point of all, the role of rate regulation in preventing insurer insolvencies. All agree that it is in the public interest to prevent the damage done by company failures; but controversy continues as to whether price competition should be restricted in order to preserve joint rate making and prevent price wars, or whether this is an unnecessary and futile application of public supervision which should be abandoned in favor of measures which seek to deal with other, presumably more realistic, causes of company insolvency.

On one point there is agreement (although each side uses the subject as an argument against the other). This is the harm, the waste, and the inefficiency involved in the current multitude of rates, forms, and rating systems. Those who favor price competition point to the impossibility of critical review by supervisory officials of the great number of filings, and the expense and political complications which ensue when the states attempt to control prices. Those who opposed price competition explain that greater uniformity is necessary in order to preserve the rating bureau system and to achieve reliable rates. The public, in the meantime, must choose blindly from among a bewildering array of alternatives each of which is reasonably priced not because competition forces it to be, but because administrative decree says it is.

The next chapter will consider price competition as a means of precluding first, excessive, and second, inadequate, automobile insurance rates.

CHAPTER V

THE EXCESSIVENESS AND ADEQUACY
STANDARDS

It is the responsibility of each insurance commissioner to see that prices charged for automobile insurance policies are neither too high nor too low. The laws of most states permit rates to be made by companies acting either jointly or independently, and, by implication, authorize price competition within a range limited by excessive and inadequate prices. There are seemingly valid reasons both for imposing stringent limitations upon price competition and thus narrowing the zone of reasonable prices, and for permitting the free play of competition within a broad range of prices. The cases favoring and opposing strict public control of competition have been presented in rather general terms; the issues will now be considered with specific reference to the standards of rate excessiveness and rate adequacy.

RATE EXCESSIVENESS

The problem faced by regulatory authorities in administering the excessiveness standard is to prevent exploitation of the public by the joint pricing system while at the same time imposing a minimum of public control over private enterprise. This calls for the striking of a balance between the goals of public protection and free enterprise, and between the methods of controlled pricing and price competition.

Interpretation of Rate Excessiveness

There probably are as many interpretations of the rate standards as there are members of the industry.[1] For purposes of convenience, they will be considered under the three-fold division used in the

[1] Gerber, Joseph E., *op. cit.*, p. 92.

previous chapter: the restrictive, permissive, and All-Industry interpretations.

The Restrictive Interpretation—It has been seen that the restrictive approach to the issue of price competition calls for membership of all companies in a single rating organization, and few, if any, deviations from a uniform rate schedule. A corollary is that bureau findings shall be paramount, it being incumbent upon all nonbureau filers to justify their departure from the bureau norm.

This interpretation, although a controversial one, is not an issue at the present time so far as the excessiveness standard is concerned, simply because the competition to bureau companies is from companies whose rates are below the bureau level (making the point relevant to the adequacy standard instead).

The Permissive Interpretation—Consistent with the permissive approach to the matter of competition, the permissive interpretation of rate excessiveness relies upon inter-company rivalry to protect the public from redundant rates.

As Moser points out, the anti-compact laws were intended to bring about free competition and to prevent price fixing and monopolization by the fire insurance companies. Because they failed to enforce competition and because some concerted rate making was in the public interest, the anti-compact laws were supplanted by rate regulatory statutes. These statutes were designed, in part, to curb the potential power of the rate-making bodies which they legalized. Had the anti-compact laws succeeded, there would have been no need for state supervision to enforce the use of reasonable rates, since competition does not permit excessive rates.[2]

From this viewpoint it follows that state regulators need not be concerned with excessiveness of nonbureau companies' rates, as there are no single automobile insurers of monopoly size.[3] Further, no question can be raised with regard to whether a company, either bureau or independent, will realize excessive profits:

> The profit a company makes should be no concern of the government so long as there are available in the area other companies willing and able to write the risk at a lesser rate. It should be the responsibility of the indi-

[2] Moser, Henry S., *op. cit.*, pp. 529–30.

[3] *Ibid.* For evaluation of this and similar assertions, see discussion below on competition as protection against excessive rates.

vidual insured to shop around for his insurance; if he wants to pay the highest price on the market, that should be his privilege, and likewise, if he wants to pay the lowest price. So long as several prices are available to choose from for the same type of insurance, no one is injured, and no one, least of all the government, should complain.[4]

The laws of California and Missouri define "excessive rates" in a manner which reflects the permissive concept:

> No rate shall be held to be excessive unless (1) such rate is unreasonably high for the insurance provided and (2) a reasonable degree of competition does not exist in the area with respect to the classification to which such rate is applicable.[5]

In Arizona, Montana, and Oklahoma also the statutes indicate that rate levels are to be presumed satisfactory if competition prevails.[6]

The Utah law is unique. Adopted in 1951, it constitutes a legislative finding of effective competition among casualty insurers in that state and says that "so long as reasonable competition continues to exist . . . no review of rates by the state is necessary or desirable." The law calls for a biennial review by the insurance commissioner to determine whether reasonable competition prevails; if it does not, provisions analogous to those in the All-Industry laws become applicable.[7]

Thus in 6 states a reasonable degree of competition is regarded as sufficient protection against the charging of excessive rates.

The All-Industry Interpretation—In one sense there is no "All-Industry interpretation" of rate excessiveness beyond the statement in the opening section of the law to the effect that it is not intended that competition be discouraged or that uniformity be either prohibited or encouraged.[8] There is no definition of "excessive rates," interpretation being left to the authorities of each state.

The following statements, however, are probably representative of the intention of most All-Industry officials. The first statement

---

[4] Matthias, Russell H., and Robison, Charles B., "State Regulation of Insurance Rates," *Insurance Law Journal*, No. 355 (August 1952), p. 541.

[5] Carlson, Thomas O., *op. cit.*, p. 58. Note that both conditions (1) and (2) must apply for a rate to be held excessive.

[6] *Ibid.*

[7] *Insurance Law Journal*, No. 388 (March 1951), p. 184. The effect of the California law is similar in that rate filings are not required, but the commissioner may at any time examine an insurer to determine whether its rates comply with the legal standards. *Insurance Hearings*, p. 4910.

[8] See discussion earlier in this chapter.

was contained in the report of a Subcommittee of the National
Association of Insurance Commissioners and refers to a memorandum submitted to it by the National Bureau of Casualty Underwriters:

> The language in the Bureau's Memorandum is to the effect that in the
> absence of a clear showing of excessiveness and unreasonableness amount-
> ing to bad faith the Bureau's proposals must be approved. Implicit in this
> is the position that, when filings are made by the Bureau, the burden of
> proof is placed upon the regulatory authority and that unless the regula-
> tory authority can sustain this burden the filing should be approved.

> It is the Subcommittee's understanding that the philosophy of the All-
> Industry Bills was to place the burden of showing that a filing meets the
> statutory standards upon the filer.[9]

The following is from a memorandum issued by the New York
Superintendent of Insurance in reference to a bill which would have
prohibited price competition in that state:

> It is well known that no matter how good state regulation of rates made by
> rating organizations composed of companies acting in concert may be, it
> is not nearly as effective in protecting the public against excessive premium
> rates as is healthy competition between "bureau companies" and independ-
> ent insurers.[10]

The intention then is to favor neither bureau filings nor independent filings, but to promote the conditions under which both
bureau and independent companies can flourish and can act as a
check against one another. There is no presumption that bureau
filings are paramount; neither is it assumed that competition will
automatically eliminate the problem of excessive rates.

Many All-Industry commissioners have found it extremely difficult to maintain the delicate balance which this policy of impar-
tiality requires. The problems are not completely dissimilar to those
involved in maintaining a balance of power among mighty nations
with conflicting philosophies. The balance seems constantly to be
slipping in one direction here and in the other direction there, and
each participant often fears that his rivals are about to get the upper
hand.

There have been frequent charges that in administering the excessiveness standard the regulatory officials have imposed a double

[9] National Association of Insurance Commissioners, *Proceedings,* 1953, p. 141.
[10] *Insurance Hearings,* p. 2148.

standard which makes it more difficult for the bureaus than for independent filers to secure approval of rate increases.[11] Occasionally the point at issue appears to be the very nature of the joint rating system.

In September 1960, for example, the Tennessee Commissioner disapproved filings by the National Bureau and N.A.U.A. for increases of 25 per cent and 6 per cent in automobile liability and physical damage rates, respectively. In doing so he said that many of the bureau companies could not as individual filers justify the increases[12] and that those few members who were fortunate enough to have had above-average experience in 1958-1959 "would be the recipient of a . . . juicy financial windfall." The bureaus, in appealing to the courts for reversal of the commissioner's order, replied that "the fact that one or more of the individual companies may have had underwriting results better than the average, while the others have had results worse than the average, is wholly irrelevant to the issue of whether the rates proposed on the basis of aggregate experience are fair, reasonable and adequate."[13]

A National Bureau filing for an automobile rate increase in Arkansas was turned down in January 1960, the Commissioner in this case also basing his action upon a fact which, from the Bureau point of view, is entirely irrelevant. He stated: "The independent filers . . . representing 69 per cent of the premium volume, are writing this class of insurance on an average of 15 per cent less than bureau rates, and they are not asking for an increase."[14]

The most celebrated case in this category was that in New York which was finally concluded in April 1959 after two years of wrangling. It began with a request by the National Bureau in the Spring of 1957 that automobile liability rates be increased 19.5 per cent. The insurance department suggested that the request be cut to 9.5 per cent; the Bureau then filed for the latter amount. The 9.5 per cent increase was refused by the commissioner in November 1957 on the grounds that it was excessive, largely because it was based upon too short an experience period.

[11] E.g., "Where's the Cheer in Chaos?" op. cit., p. 9.
[12] The National Underwriter, October 14, 1960, p. 4.
[13] Ibid., October 21, 1960, p. 41.
[14] Ibid., February 5, 1960, p. 13.

In department hearings of the case, the Bureau brought out the following points: (1) member companies had sustained a 10.1 per cent or $24.1 million underwriting loss in New York during 1956, (2) the two-year experience period upon which the filing was based had been used in New York and throughout the country for 30 years and was identical to the period used by Allstate in filing for a 12.9 per cent increase which the department had approved in September 1957, (3) the filing incorporated a reduction in production cost allowance from 25 per cent to 20 per cent, and (4) a 3.5 per cent profit provision was used in computing the rates, although a 5 per cent figure was used in 47 other states and territories.[15]

Following the hearing, the department for the second time rejected the proposed 9.5 per cent increase in January 1958. The Bureau appealed the decision, and in June 1958 the court annulled the commissioner's disapproval. The court stated that application of the tests of rate reasonableness required the exercise of judgment and that it would not challenge the commissioner's judgment in calling for a longer experience period,

> But it went on to say that it is clear, however, that if the application of any standard, however reasonable in general concept it may seem will cause an illegal and unreasonable result in a particular case, the principle of administrative discretion in the formulation of standards does not render that result invulnerable to attack. The crux of this case is not the propriety, as an abstract proposition, of one rate making basis or another, but is, rather, the question whether the rates which remain in force by reason of the disapproval of the revisions are in fact adequate and those proposed unreasonable.[16]

The court ruled that there was not sufficient evidence to support the commissioner's disapproval of the rate filing.

In the elections of November 1958, the incumbent Democratic state administration was defeated. Decision on the last filing having been delayed by further court action, the Bureau made a new filing on December 3rd; this time requesting a 40 per cent increase. The latter filing was disapproved in February 1959.[17]

[15] *Ibid.*, January 10, 1958, p. 35.

[16] *Ibid.*, June 27, 1958, pp. 27–8.

[17] It was pointed out in the press at the time that the new Republican state administration was trying to get a tax increase through the legislature, and it was suggested that "approval by the administration of an increase in rates on liability on automobiles, which concerns so many citizens of the state, is not likely—at least until the tax revision is put out of the way." *The National Underwriter,* February 13, 1959, p. 38.

The case was finally brought to a close in April 1959 when the insurance department approved an 18.4 per cent rate increase.

The New York case illustrates several of the problems of the All-Industry approach to automobile rate regulation. First, the circumstances and timing gave rise to charges that the cause of proper rate regulation had been subverted to the expediency of practical politics.[18]

It also illustrates the delay which insurers must sometimes endure before securing approval of a needed increase. The rates finally approved were almost identical with those originally requested two years previously. In the interim, bureau companies sustained staggering losses on automobile insurance in New York State.[19]

This dispute also illustrates the difficulty of applying any fixed tests of rate reasonableness. In annulling the New York commissioner's disapproval of the filing, the court did not question his authority to require the use of more than two years' experience. It was pointed out, however, that if the current rates were assumed to have been reasonable when they were approved, and if losses had since increased (a fact not challenged by the department), then those rates could no longer be adequate. The court was not concerned with the commissioner's method of evaluating the filing, but only with the *result*.[20] Thus any interpretation or test of the rate standards which an All-Industry commissioner might apply would be valid only so long as the results in a specific case were reasonable.

Finally, the New York case exemplifies the circumstances which cause allegations that a double standard is applied in interpretating rate excessiveness. In departmental hearings on the 9.5 per cent filing, counsel for the National Bureau said it was unfair and illegal for the superintendent to apply one set of standards for one company (Allstate) and another set for other companies (bureau members).[21]

---

[18] *E.g.*, Statement of: Crafts, James F., National Association of Insurance Commissioners, *Proceedings*, 1958, p. 226; Force, Kenneth O., "Regulation is Asked for What It Can't be Expected to Deliver," *The National Underwriter*, May 9, 1958, pp. 1, ff.

[19] Underwriting losses were $65 million in 1957 and probably more than that amount in 1958. *The National Underwriter*, April 3, 1959, p. 1.

[20] *Ibid.*, June 27, 1958, pp. 27–8.

[21] *Ibid.*, January 10, 1958, p. 35.

It may be that the All-Industry law philosophy of complete neutrality between bureau and independent filings is impossible to carry out; the issues may be too closely related to one's personal economic and political philosophy. The diversity of interpretations among the All-Industry commissioners would seem to indicate that each has a bias no matter how conscientious he may be. The rate standards are in fact construed so many different ways that each independent company and each rating organization must employ an expert on filings just to keep track of "all of these vagaries of interpretation."[22]

These difficulties in applying the All-Industry laws have led many company and state officials to the conclusion that the tests applied by the regulators to determine whether specific rates are inadequate or excessive should be made more concrete.[23] The tests of excessiveness which have been proposed are along the lines of the California definition, relating this standard to the existing degree of competition.[24]

It, therefore, is suitable to inquire whether competition is a feasible test of rate excessiveness, and what the result of applying this test to automobile insurance would be.

Competition as a Test of Rate Excessiveness

According to the California-type definition, rates cannot be excessive if "a reasonable degree of competition" prevails in the market for the particular kind of insurance. The questions which immediately arise are: What constitutes a sufficient amount of competition to preclude excessive rates, and how can the state insurance department determine whether or not this reasonable degree of competition exists?

Clearly, the economists' theoretical models of pure and perfect competition are not appropriate. These are tools of theoretical analysis which define the conditions necessary to achieve a long-run equilibrium with equality between prices and costs. The conditions of pure and perfect competition, including perfect substitutability

---

[22] Carlson, Thomas O., *op. cit.,* p. 19.

[23] National Association of Insurance Commissioners, "Report of Subcommittee to Review Fire and Casualty Rating Laws and Regulations," [1960], p. 4. (Mimeographed.)

[24] See *The National Underwriter,* May 26, 1961, p. 48.

and knowledge and complete freedom of entry, are not intended to constitue a description of reality.

Likewise, the model of monopolistic competition is impractical as a basis for administering the rate regulatory laws. Its assumption of constant costs and free entry at costs identical to those of existing firms provides conditions under which an industry could theoretically attain long-run equilibrium without monopoly profit and with price exceeding minimum average cost. This concept and that of pure and perfect competition facilitate the study of real situations by directing attention to the ways in which actual markets deviate in form and results from certain abstract constructions; they are not suitable, however, as guides to public policy.

A more practical basis for rate regulation is provided by the concept of workable competition, which attempts to identify the conditions likely to bring the desired results of pure competition without the rigidly assumed structure and theoretical refinements of the competitive models. The term "workable competition" was introduced by J. M. Clark in 1940.[25] Since then there has been much discussion of the concept by economists and many differing presentations of it. One such presentation is that adopted by the Attorney General's National Committee to Study the Antitrust Laws.[26] This conceptualization will serve as the basis of the present analysis.

According to the Committee, "the economic definition of workable competition concentrates on the effective limits it sets on the power of a seller, or group of sellers acting in concert, over their price." Ten factors are listed which are "considered some of the more important" in determining whether workable competition exists. They relate to: (1) number of sellers, (2) entry, (3) independence of rivals, (4) preclusive practices, (5) growth, (6) incentives to competitive moves, (7) product differentiation, (8) pricing, (9) excess capacity, and (10) price discrimination. The Committee noted that the first three are the most important.

Each of the 10 factors will be applied to the automobile insur-

[25] Clark, J. M., "Toward a Concept of Workable Competition," *American Economic Review*, Vol. XXX, No. 2 (June 1940).

[26] *Report*, Attorney General's National Committee to Study the Antitrust Laws (Washington: U. S. Government Printing Office, 1955). Quotations in this section are from pp. 324–36 of this Report unless otherwise noted.

ance market. It should be recognized that "there are no objective criteria of workable competition, and such criteria as are proffered are at best intuitively reasonable modifications of the rigorous and abstract criteria of perfect competition."[27] The criteria do provide a framework, however, which aids in the judging of the extent to which competitive pressures preclude the establishment of excessive prices.

"A Number of Effective Sellers: The Issue of Relative Size"

> Absolute size . . . has no significance in determining the presence or absence of workable competition. . . . For effective competition . . . there should be that degree of self-interested independent rivalry in any given market that exists where there is no one firm or group of firms acting in concert which . . . could hold for long the power to choose its level of profits by giving less and charging more. . . . Rivalry should not depend entirely upon sellers who are so weak or inefficient as to exist by sufferance. For such firms are not independent, and are not properly counted among the number of effectively competitive sellers.

With many thousands of agents selling automobile insurance policies on behalf of over 600 companies, it is obvious that there is a sufficient number of sellers to make competition workable. Furthermore, many of the insurers which are small on a national scale are significant factors and sometimes leaders in a particular state.[28] Among the big companies, absence of substantial concentration of power is indicated by the fact that the 20 largest earn less than half of the annual premiums.[29]

It cannot be overlooked, however, that many automobile insurers do not engage in completely independent rivalry. The significance of this point will be considered shortly.

"Opportunity for Entry"

> Relative freedom of opportunity for entry of new rivals is a fundamental requisite for effective competition in the long run. . . . The entry and withdrawal of firms . . . is the basic mechanism of the market for achieving its economic results.

It was seen previously that there are no major obstacles to the entry of new firms into the automobile insurance market.[30] The in-

---

[27] *Ibid.*, p. 339.
[28] See discussion of company size and concentration in Chapter II.
[29] Above, Table 10.
[30] See discussion of entry in Chapter II.

ability of existing insurers to prevent the establishment of alternate sources of supply is one of the most significant competitive aspects of the market.

Withdrawal of existing firms from the market, on the other hand, is impeded by regulations which attempt to prevent company insolvencies. If the market were dominated by bureau companies and if the supervisory officials refused to approve any rate below the level needed to sustain the least efficient insurer, the result could conceivably be a general redundancy in the rates charged by all companies or at least by the bureau members. The market is not controlled by the rating bureaus though, except in those states where membership is mandatory. Even in those states, there is no evidence that rate levels are excessive. Barriers to exit from the market are more pertinent to the adequacy than to the excessiveness standard.

"Independence of Rivals"

> A primary condition of workable competition . . . is that there be genuine independence on the part of the business units in an industry, so that each firm pursues its own individual advantage.

This is perhaps the key point in evaluating the effectiveness of competition in automobile insurance. Bureau companies of course do not pursue independent pricing policies. Exemptions from federal and state antitrust laws permit them to engage in practices which in other industries would be termed collusive and monopolistic.

Because concerted pricing has been legalized and because of the supply and demand conditions which prevail, rating bureaus *could* exploit their position at the expense of the policy buying public. That is, with a relatively elastic supply and inelastic demand,[31] a slight restriction in the amount of insurance offered would permit a substantial increase in rate levels.[32] The ability of rating organizations to follow the monopolistic policy of "choosing their level of profits by giving less and charging more" is one reason why state supervision is essential. Prosecution of the South-Eastern Under-

---

[31] See Chapter II, sections on demand and supply.

[32] This can be visualized as the results of an upward shift of an almost horizontal supply curve which intersects with an almost vertical demand curve. The new intersection will be at a point of slightly less quantity, but substantially higher price.

writers Association case revealed that the fire insurance companies were pursuing such practices in the early 1940's. This, however, was prior to adoption of the McCarran Act and the present rate regulatory laws. And in passing the McCarran Act, Congress stipulated that the Sherman Anti-Trust Act would continue to apply with respect to boycott, coercion and intimidation,[33] thus barring the use of these practices to consolidate bureau control of insurance markets.[34]

Although it is conceivable that those companies which set rates in concert could secure and exploit monopolistic control of automobile insurance, it is clear that they are not attempting to control the industry and probably could not do so at the present time. Bureau companies are making no effort to exclude competitors, divide the market among themselves, restrict supply and behave in the manner of a monopolist. Rating bureaus do not provide price leadership for the rest of the industry; rather, member companies for several years have been seeking means to halt the loss of their customers to rival insurers selling at lower prices.

Furthermore, there is vigorous competition among the members of the rating organizations. As the Merritt Committee said, bureaus are not trusts. While their members do not usually compete on the basis of price, nonprice competition is strong.

Finally, bureau companies do not dominate the automobile insurance market. Tables 7 and 8 (Chapter II) show that all of the bureau members and subscriber companies together write less than one-half of the business. In some respects (including pricing) it would not be amiss to consider this an oligopolistic market, even though it includes several hundred separate firms. Great numbers of these firms are either bureau members which make pricing decisions in conjunction with fellow members, or are companies too small to develop innovations and merchandise them effectively. The number of effective decision-making units in this sense is small, consisting of the major bureaus and perhaps 6 large independent companies. This is few enough that an important competitive move

[33] Section 3.

[34] Several cases have been brought by the Department of Justice under this section of the McCarran Act. See Hansen, Victor R., "Insurance Competition and the Antitrust Laws," *Insurance Law Journal*, No. 418 (November 1957).

by any one unit may affect the sales of the others to such an extent that readjustments will be made by the latter.

Because of the substantial resources and competitive stature of these larger units, competition among them in some respects may be more effective than among a great number of individual companies. It appears that most of the important competitive moves in the industry are made by one or more of these units either in anticipation of or in response to action by the others.

To the extent that independent rivalry among bureau companies is lacking, effective competition exists between the bureaus and the major nonbureau insurers. At the same time, each individual bureau company seeks to promote its own advantage. It is concluded that, through the combination of these forces, sufficient independent rivalry presently exists so that this test of workable competition is met by the automobile insurance market.

"Predatory Preclusive Practices"

> There should be no predatory preclusive tactics, such that their natural effect would be to enable the user to eliminate rivals without regard to their efficiency, or at least to place them under serious handicaps irrelevant to their efficiency. It should be noted as a practical matter that predatory competition in this sense can usually only be waged where a considerable degree of market power already exists, or where an attempt is being made to use a long purse in order to destroy or coerce rivals.

It was pointed out earlier[35] that, although certain rating bureaus used such tactics prior to 1945, legislation adopted since that time renders these examples obsolete.

The only thing which might be considered a predatory preclusive practice at this time is the alleged market creaming: securing new business by writing it at a rate which the insurer knows to be inadequate and later either raising the rate or retaining only the above-average risks.[36] In order to secure permanently the advantage thus obtained, however, the company would need to dominate the market, something which no automobile insurer now does. Additionally, as the Attorney General's Committee pointed out, accusations of predatory or cutthroat practices often actually stem not from the abuse of significant degrees of market power, but from the uncom-

---

[35] Chapters II and III.
[36] Cf. Chapter IV, section discussing "market creaming."

fortably active pressures of competition itself. If such practices actually did exist, there is no reason to presume they would not come to the attention of the regulatory officials who are in a position to halt them.

"Rate of Growth of the Industry or Market"

> The speed with which an industry is growing is not a direct economic indicator of the state of competition within it. An industry may be actually in decline and yet be effectively competitive. . . . Rate of growth, however, is often important in determining the significance to be attached to other factors, and particularly to numbers and reasonable opportunity for entry.

While there are many individual exceptions, the insurance industry as a whole has never been notoriously progressive. It has a reputation (perhaps undeserved) of inadequate employment standards and low salary scales.[37] It lags far behind many industries in the support of basic research.[38] The charge has even been made that "the soaring imagination is suspect in insurance."[39] Among powerful agency groups it too often appears that company proposals of new and more efficient methods are opposed mainly for the sake of opposing change.[40]

On the other hand, the industry has provided the greatly increased capacity needed for the insurance of our growing population and expanding usage of motor vehicles. And significantly it has done so in a competitive atmosphere which has "created both an opportunity and a necessity for managements to become more efficient, reduce operating costs, correct unsound practices and develop competitive rating plans and new policies."[41] This growth and change make it possible for firms to expand without imposing losses upon their rivals, and inject elements of uncertainty which frustrate attempts to monopolize the market.

[37] *The National Underwriter,* February 14, 1958, p. 6.

[38] *Ibid.,* p. 35.

[39] "The Underwriters," *op. cit.,* p. 108.

[40] *E.g.,* see Kenney, Roger, "A Local Agent Sets Forth His Creed on Meeting Specialty Company Competition," *United States Investor,* February 27, 1961, p. 29; Bandy, Joe H., "The Automobile Situation," *Best's Insurance News,* November 1955, p. 20; also Gerber, Joseph S., "An Agent's Position in a Rate Regulatory System," *Insurance Law Journal,* No. 460 (May 1961). Commissioner Gerber says "the state of mind of the agency system is sickly. It is not geared for the bright future."

[41] *Best's Insurance Reports (Fire and Casualty)* (New York: Alfred M. Best Co., 1960). p. ix.

"Character of Market Incentives to Competitive Moves"

> In general, . . . effective competition may hinge on the condition that the
> initiator of a competitive action can expect a gain in volume of business
> at least for a time. That is, the customers' response to an inducement may
> be quicker than rivals' responses for at least long enough to provide a pay-
> out period for the competitive action.

The most notable instance of gain through competitive action
in the automobile insurance market is that achieved by the direct-
writing companies. The innovation which they sponsored was nothing less than a revolution in the system of marketing the product.
For more than a decade these companies reaped the benefit of their
move almost at will. Now it appears that the traditional agency
system is being modified in the ways necessary to meet the direct-
writers' competition.

Most of the innovations in this field in recent years are attributable directly or indirectly to nonbureau companies.[42] Kulp remarked
that "to the spur of the independent and to the open or implicit
threat of the more independent-minded bureau members to resign
when bureau agreements and policies seem restrictive, must be
credited most new ideas (good or bad) in casualty insurance."[43] But
bureau companies also have been able to benefit from competitive
moves, one example being merit rating (See Chapter II) which,
after a number of unsuccessful attempts, now seems to be winning
back for the member companies some of the business previously
lost to their direct-writing rivals.[44]

It should be noted that because of the strategic position of the
salesman in this industry, many of the competitive moves seek to
win or retain his favor and thus to increase company sales indirectly.
Competition in the form of contingent commission contracts, cooperative company-agency advertising and more efficient application
and claim processing add to the effectiveness of competition even
though the public may not be aware of such actions.

[42] For a list of the changes inaugurated by independent companies, see Mertz, Arthur
C., *op. cit.*, p. 132.

[43] Kulp, C. A., "The Rate-Making Process in Property and Casualty Insurance—Goals,
Technics, and Limits," *Law and Contemporary Problems*, Vol. XV, No. 4 (Autumn 1950),
p. 513.

[44] *The Wall Street Journal*, January 25, 1961, p. 1; *The National Underwriter*, June 2,
1961, p. 24.

In those states where rating bureaus do not completely dominate,[45] the incentive to competitive moves is sufficient to meet this test of workable competition.

"Product Differentiation and Product Homogeneity"

> If other conditions are equal, . . . the more homogeneous the product of rival sellers, the more easily buyers could switch from the output of one competitor to that of others; and therefore the wider the market and the greater the degree of competition in it. . . . Relatively mild differentiation of products within a market otherwise effectively competitive, however, may be a factor favorable to the intensiveness of competition. . . . This will tend to be most forcibly the case if the product differentiation reflects product rivalry, that is, product improvement, rather than mere heterogeneity of closely similar products.

The subject of product differentiation in automobile insurance was discussed in some detail in the previous chapter.[46] There are few obstacles to independent product modification or to the imitation of rivals' innovations other than the restrictions imposed by state regulation. Product heterogeneity is extensive, but for the most part does not represent true product rivalry and improvement. In the writer's opinion, much product differentiation in the field is superfluous; "mere heterogeneity of closely similar products." Competition would be more effective if differentiation were controlled to the point that consumers could choose rationally among a restricted number of recognizably different products.

"Meeting or Matching the Prices of Rivals"

> It is of the essence of effective competition that competitors should try to meet, or offer an equivalent for, any superior inducement which one of them offers. Meeting a rival's inducements is the means whereby competition diffuses the gains of productive efficiency. . . . Effective competition also involves freedom to undercut rivals' prices. . . . Any rule, public or private, which forbade the meeting of prices, or one which forbade the undercutting of prices, would be a rule against workable competition.

There is vigorous price competition for automobile insurance in all of the states where independent pricing is permitted. In those states, there are continuous efforts to meet or undercut rivals' prices. Therefore, the legalization of joint pricing need not and does not foreclose workable competition as long as it is on a voluntary basis.

[45] Note the case of Texas (Chapter IV).
[46] See Chapter IV, on excessive number of rates and forms.

The Committee mentioned elsewhere that "reduction of costs and moderation of profits . . . do not prove the existence, nor their absence the lack, of effective competition." It is entirely possible for a monopolistic industry to have a better record in these respects than a competitive industry. At the same time, it is a sound assumption that "competition will on the average result in much more progressiveness and efficiency than monopoly."

While not conclusive as evidence of competition, the available data do not indicate excessive costs or profits in automobile insurance. Although the cost of the coverage has risen in recent years, it has been remarked that "the automobile insurance premium is the spout of a funnel into which are poured a witch's mixture of irresponsible driving, big jury awards, high lawyer's fees, rising hospital and doctors' bills, inadequate and improper roads, poor or inadequate enforcement, and plain skullduggery by a few garages, motor car dealers, lawyers, doctors, and insurance company personnel."[47]

The cost reducing innovations pioneered by the direct writing companies have given them a marked competitive advantage which has put pressure upon bureau companies to reduce their costs. In addition to this pressure, Zoffer points out that the bureau rating system involves a ratchet effect which exerts a constant downward pressure upon bureau company expenses:

> Since the expense allowances are developed from a compilation of the expense figures of the individual companies, competition tends to lower the adjustable expenses to a minimum. Each carrier will attempt to reduce expenses so that they will be below the Bureau allowance and thus enable the individual carrier to maximize profits. This minimizing of expenses, however, will affect the next rate revision, when the reduced expenses are reported to the Bureau. Companies will reduce expenses until their ability to reduce below the Bureau allowance is negligible, at which time an attempt is made to keep expenses at approximately the Bureau levels.[48]

Expense reductions adopted in recent years include commission reductions by most of the American agency system companies. For their part many agents, although resisting certain expense reducing innovations through their associations, are individually adopting

---

[47] Force, Kenneth O., "Auto Is More Complex, Competitive," *The National Underwriter*, June 10, 1960, p. 42. It was stated in 1958 that during the previous five years hospital expenses increased 33 per cent, medical care 17 per cent, auto repairs 19 per cent and automobile liability rates only 9.3 per cent. *Ibid.*, November 28, 1958, p. 7.

[48] Zoffer, *op. cit.*, p. 177.

lower-cost methods of operation. For example, over one-half of the members of the National Association of Insurance Agents are already using or planning to use continuous policies and direct premium billing.[49]

It is reported that "competition is exerting tremendous downward pressure on profit margins, even before normal profit margins exist."[50] In the decade of the 1950's, 10 of the most prosperous years our economy has known, stock and mutual companies managed to earn an underwriting profit of only 1.6 per cent (617 million) on $38.4 billion in automobile insurance earned premiums.[51]

What Adam Smith wrote almost 200 years ago is probably true in this field today: "Though many people have made a little money by insurance, very few have made a great fortune; and from this consideration alone, it seems evident enough, that the ordinary balance of profit and loss is not more advantageous in this, than in other common trades."[52]

"Excess Capacity"

If the companies in an industry tend generally to pursue policies of making more money by charging high prices and restricting production, the industry may have chronic excess capacity as a result.

Excess capacity is not a characteristic of the automobile insurance business. To the contrary, the companies at times have been hard pressed to provide sufficient capacity.[53]

"Price Discrimination"

Some types of price discrimination may stimulate effective competition; others may be evidence of effective monopoly.

Price discrimination is inherent to the pooling and insuring of risks. In addition, certain forms of unfair price competition (such as rebating) exist. Such practices are prohibited by the rating laws, and Williams concluded that "the administration of the statutes has been for the most part conscientious and competent, considering

[49] Force, Kenneth O., *The National Underwriter,* September 30, 1960, p. 8.
[50] *Best's Insurance Reports (Fire and Casualty)* (New York: Alfred M. Best Co., 1961). p. ix.
[51] Computed from *Best's Fire and Casualty Aggregates and Averages, op. cit.,* pp. 142 and 209.
[52] Smith, Adam, *The Wealth of Nations* (Modern Library ed., New York: Random House, 1937), p. 108.
[53] Chapter II, section on conditions of supply of automobile insurance.

the limited budgets that have been made available by state legislatures . . . ."[54] There is no indication that price discrimination in automobile insurance makes competition unworkable.

The Workability of Competition

The majority of the tests of workable competition are met by the automobile insurance industry without question or qualification. There are more than enough sellers; entry is sufficiently free; the rate of growth is satisfactory; there is plenty of incentive to competitive moves; the companies attempt to meet or undercut rivals' prices; and neither excess capacity nor price discrimination is a problem.

On the score of independent rivalry, bureau companies could monopolize the market under some circumstances, but are not presently trying to do so, and could not do so under present conditions. The predatory preclusive practice of market creaming is a possibility in the absence of rate regulation and is sometimes alleged to be a current practice. Finally, product differentiation is excessive, although this is probably not a decisive impediment to workable competition.[55]

On the basis of this analysis the conclusion is reached that currently, there is workable competition in automobile insurance. Competitive pressures will prevent the maintenance of excessive price levels; public control to prevent the use of excessive rates is unnecessary except on a stand-by basis. Therefore, inclusion in the insurance laws of a statement to the effect that rates shall not be deemed excessive so long as workable competition prevails would be in the public interest. Such a statement would focus attention upon the logical and historical purpose of the excessiveness standard and would provide a guide for its application. So long as present competitive conditions persisted, detailed scrutiny of rate filings for the purpose of guarding against excessive rates could therefore largely be dispensed with.

It should be pointed out that the stipulation relating rate excessiveness to the absence of workable competition would not limit

54 Williams, C. Arthur, op. cit., p. 96.
55 Control of both product differentiation and market creaming relate to the adequacy standard which is discussed in the remainder of this chapter.

the authority of the insurance commissioners if positive regulation became truly necessary; the laws would still prohibit the use of excessive rates. The provision would, however, remove what sometimes have been unnecessary restraints upon the functioning of free enterprise in the insurance business.

RATE ADEQUACY

The most vital goal of insurance rate regulation is the protection of company solvency. The chief problem of the supervisory officials in administering the requirement of rate adequacy is to prevent the use of rates which would threaten company financial strength while at the same time imposing a minimum of public control over company operation. Rates driven to low levels by competitive pressures are in the public interest only if they are not so low that insurers are unable, in the long run, to maintain solvency and pay losses. Public regulation must seek a proper balance between the advantages of free competition and the public protection afforded by the control of competition.

Interpretations of Rate Adequacy

As is the case with the excessiveness standard, most insurance laws simply require that rates not be "inadequate," but do not define the term. And again the result has been a diversity of interpretations among the various states. Whitney says that "in some states and on some classes of risk it is said that a deviation can be accomplished, if no objection is raised, by a 'postcard to the commissioner'—who is very likely delighted to have a rate move downward."[56] In other instances deviations are seldom or never permitted.

The Restrictive Interpretation—The restrictive interpretation of rate adequacy is summarized in the following statement:

> Now adequacy for rate-making purposes is determined by taking the aggregate loss experience of the carriers concerned, and the aggregate expenses, and comparing the result with the rates. It cannot be done, company by company, for the experience of a single company is from the statistical standpoint inadequate as a true criterion for the future.[57]

[56] Whitney, Simon, *op. cit.,* p. 353.
[57] Hobbs, Clarence W., "State Regulation of Insurance Rates," 1925, p. 272.

The essence of this position is the belief that price competition in insurance will drive rates too low and that company solvency will be defended by enforcing price uniformity. This and the other arguments for restricting competition which were presented in the previous chapter are the reasons why rate reductions by individual companies are resisted in certain jurisdictions.

The Permissive Interpretation—At the other extreme are those interpretations which hold that, in the absence of threats to competition or to company solvency or profits, rate adequacy should be of no concern to government. This attitude was expressed by an Allstate official in the following statement:

> An insurer or bureau should be permitted to experiment and progress, based upon its sound and properly exercised and supported judgment. Certainly in the case of an individual insurer, if it is solvent and the proposed experiment does not threaten its solvency, there exists no public interest requiring the disapproval of such filing, even though supported entirely by judgment. The company has the ability to remain solvent and pay its claims and after credible experience becomes available, the filing can be re-examined in the light of such experience. If the filing later proves unsound, no harm has been done to the public.[58]

This concept of adequacy assumes that rate wars and threats to insolvency (while highly unlikely), could be detected by means other than scrutiny of rate filings, such as by review of (1) loss and expense data filed annually by each company, (2) annual company statements, and (3) the periodic convention examination reports.[59]

The argument is also made that the attempt to justify uniform rate laws on the ground that they are needed to protect company solvency "smacks of a suggestion that inefficient or economically unsound ventures should be shielded from the probing fingers of healthy competition."[60] It is held that "such a suggestion profanes the whole philosophy of our business economy and the spirit of our Federal and State antitrust laws."[61]

The laws of several states explicitly define rate inadequacy in terms of either competition, company profits, or company solvency. The effect is a liberalization of regulatory control over price competition. These definitions are considered later in this chapter.

[58] Kline, George H., *op. cit.*, p. 52.
[59] Moser, Henry S., "Operation of Independents . . ." p. 536.
[60] Statement of Vestal Lemmon, *Insurance Hearings*, p. 1228.
[61] *Ibid.*

The All-Industry Interpretation—Interpretation of the adequacy standard in the remaining states is left to the judgment of the commissioner. As with the excessiveness standard, the result has been considerable variation among the states. At one extreme are constructions like that of the Connecticut commissioner who requested of Allstate "loss and expense data justifying the differential between your rates and those of the National Bureau companies."[62] In contrast is a statement of the Kentucky Court of Appeals: "We find ourselves in agreement with the basic tenet of the company's position, which is that an insurer's solvency is a dominating consideration in the regulation of its rates, and that a rate structure is adequate if the insurer is financially able to furnish sound insurance and to meet its obligations."[63]

Such differences in interpretation have brought from both sides charges that a double standard is used by the regulatory officials in determining the adequacy of filed rates. Independent companies claim that they have been subjected to a deliberate campaign of harassment to prevent them from using competitive rates,[64] while bureau companies allege that their proposals for rate reductions are given closer scrutiny than those of independents.[65]

The Need for Regulation of Rate Adequacy

In view of the differing interpretations of the adequacy standard, it seems appropriate to review the purposes and the need for this type of control. There are several possible objectives of the requirement that rates be adequate, the most important of which is generally considered to be the protection of insurer solvency. It is likely that the disputes over administration of the standard stem from disagreement on (1) the likelihood of competitive rates causing insolvencies, (2) the historical record of such failures, (3) the ability of rate regulation to handle this problem, and (4) the use of the adequacy standard as a means of achieving objectives other than the preservation of insurer solvency.

There seem to be rather strong theoretical grounds for believing

[62] "Allstate Filing Criticized," *United States Investor*, May 2, 1959, p. 8.
[63] The case related to a fire insurance deviation filed by Meridian Mutual, *The National Underwriter*, March 31, 1961, p. 8.
[64] McHugh, Donald P., "Rate Regulation Revisited," p. 103.
[65] "Where's the Cheer in Chaos?" *Journal of American Insurance*, January 1961, p. 9.

that unrestrained price competition would force rates below the level of adequacy. This reasoning is based upon the fact that the full cost of an automobile policy is not known at the time it is sold, and the feeling that under competitive pressures company executives would be prone to under-estimate future losses. It is also based upon the testimony of actuaries that individual companies, unless of very great size, do not have an adequate statistical basis for the determination of reliable rates.

But the actual record of insurer insolvencies fails to confirm the deductive determination that failures are likely to be caused by low rates. There is no evidence that a single automobile insurer (or other property-casualty company) has failed for several decades as a result of using inadequate rates. Many companies have failed during that period, but the unanimous testimony[66] of those who are familiar with these cases is that they are attributable to factors other than low rates.[67]

There is in fact evidence that rate regulation, rather than guaranteeing the financial stability of insurance carriers, has been at least a partial cause of some company losses. In the 10-year period 1951-1960, the stock companies sustained an $809 million loss on automobile bodily injury liability coverage. Total premium earned during the period was $12.6 billion; underwriting losses were sustained in every year except 1953 and 1954.[68] The companies were of course aware of the need for higher rate levels, but their requests for approval of increases were repeatedly rejected or delayed.

Furthermore, the record in those states where rate adequacy is not closely supervised has been fully as good as in the states which have insisted upon detailed statistical justification of rate reductions. Rate wars have not developed in the permissive states and insurers have not been driven into insolvency.

The insurance commissioners of California and Missouri, where not only is adequacy defined in a permissive manner but no rate

66 *Cf* Chapter IV, section discussing company failures.

67 It does not appear reasonable to give state regulation full credit for this record because (1) in most states regulatory laws had not been adopted during a large part of this period, (2) regulation is still ineffective in some states because of inadequate budgets and staffs, and (3) regulatory policies differ widely among the states which do have adequate resources.

68 *Best's Fire and Casualty Aggregates and Averages. op. cit.,* p. 144.

filings are required, both have stated that their laws are operating satisfactorily and are in the public interest.[69] The commissioner of Idaho, where filings are not currently required because of a finding that reasonable competition exists, also reports no insolvency problems and general satisfaction with the effectiveness of automobile rate regulation.[70]

Finally, rate regulation is clearly incapable of preventing insolvencies. In this regard, the following comment was made by former Superintendent Vorys of Ohio:

> Who knows whether a rate is really adequate? . . . Adequacy for one company will not necessarily constitute adequacy for another. It varies with a company's loss ratio, expense factor, the nature of its agency force, its underwriting ability and the conservatism of its management. The purpose of requiring adequacy is solvency. I question whether the finding of adequacy in a rate accomplishes such high purpose when there is no guarantee of the adequacy of the underwriter.[71]

The conclusion is reached that while there is in theory a likelihood that price competition will cause insolvencies, such has not been the result in practice and that further, the insolvencies which have occurred are not attributable to the use of low rates.

It does not follow, however, that public control of rate adequacy should be abandoned completely. Even though the danger of low rates causing insolvencies has often been over-emphasized, government has a responsibility to see that the theoretical possibility does not become a reality. The stakes are too great to permit the abdication of this responsibility; there is not a person in the country who, either as an insured or as a potential claimant, does not have a direct interest in the ability of automobile insurers to meet their commitments. Some form of government rate regulation to protect this interest is mandatory.

Several other reasons why control of rate adequacy may be necessary were revealed in the previous discussion of the excessiveness standard. These are (1) the alleged practice of setting unfair "cut-rate" prices on automobile insurance in a manner calculated to skim the most attractive risks from the market, (2) the presence of need-

[69] Insurance Hearings, pp. 4750 and 4755.
[70] Letter from Commissioner Leo O'Connell, June 5, 1961.
[71] Vorys, Arthur I., "The Responsibilities of the Insurance Commissioner," Papers and Proceedings, National Association of Mutual Insurance Companies, October 1957, p. 75.

less and harmful product differentiation, and (3) the challenge of low-rate insurers to the survival of the joint pricing system. The need for preventing market creaming and excessive product differentiation was made apparent in the previous discussion. The need to protect the rating bureaus from low-rate price competition is not evaluated in this study.

In summary, regulation of rate adequacy in automobile insurance might have one or more of the following objectives: (1) protection of insurer solvency, (2) prevention of unfair pricing practices (market creaming), (3) restriction of product differentiation, and (4) preservation of the rating bureau system.

Excluding from consideration the last of these four objectives, the problem is to determine the degree of restraint upon price competition which is necessary to furnish the required protection to the public. Since it has been concluded that the danger of destructive price warfare in automobile insurance has been exaggerated (and since it has been assumed that governmental control should be limited to the amount of regulation required for proper public protection), the most satisfactory answer to the problem may lie in one of the permissive definitions of rate adequacy.

Tests of Rate Adequacy

The laws of California, Idaho, Missouri and Oklahoma state that:

> No rate shall be held to be inadequate unless (1) such rate is unreasonably low for the insurance provided, and (2) the continued use of such rate endangers the solvency of the insurer using the same, or unless (3) such rate is unreasonably low for the insurance provided and the use of such rate by the insurer using same has, or if continued will have, the effect of destroying competition or creating a monopoly.

In Arizona, Minnesota and Rhode Island rates cannot be held inadequate if the coverage is being written by the filing company at a profit. The Montana and Nebraska statutes say that rates are not inadequate unless their use endangers the solvency of the company using them. Utah defines inadequacy in terms of competition, as well as profits and solvency.[72]

These various tests of rate adequacy rely upon one or more of

[72] Carlson, Thomas O., *op. cit.*, p. 56-8.

three factors: destruction of competition, company solvency, and company profits. The feasibility of each will be considered.

Destruction of Competition—The California law, among others, says that rates are inadequate if their use will destroy competition or create a monopoly. This does not seem a suitable approach in view of the objectives of regulation as they have been defined.

Monopolization of the automobile insurance business is not currently a danger. In the words of Commissioner McConnell of California, "There has never existed, and I think there will never exist, a single insurer so vast of resources and with a management so scheming and patient to curb and defer their quest of profit so that that company would use unreasonably low rates until it threatened to destroy competition or create a monopoly."[73]

In addition, it would be difficult or impossible for insurance departments to identify those rates which did not meet this test of adequacy (and prove that they did not) until after the damage had been done and competitors had been destroyed. While it is possible to make a judgment of when workable competition ceases to exist, it is another matter to forecast or even identify the effect of a particular rate upon the competitive environment of an industry.

Company Solvency—Several states define an inadequate rate as one which endangers the solvency of the company using it. Superintendent Leggett of Missouri whose law contains this test has said:

> We can readily determine whether or not the rates charged by a particular company are inadequate by an examination of the annual statement of that company. If the rates charged produce an income insufficient to sustain the solvency of the company we have authority under the statute to correct that situation.[74]

It has, however, been seen that it is seldom low rates that are the cause of insurer insolvencies. Financial difficulties may be brought on by any one of a countless number of factors. To force a company which is in trouble to use higher rates when the trouble was not caused by inadequate ones would be likely to aggravate the problem.

Because solvency is affected by so many things, application of this test would needlessly complicate rate regulation. As with the

[73] *Insurance Hearings*, p. 4752.
[74] *Ibid.*, pp. 1205–6.

test based on destruction of competition, it would be extremely difficult for an insurance department to sustain its position when disapprovals based upon this definition were appealed to the courts. Rate regulation would continue to vary among the states, depending in each upon the judgment of the supervisory officials. The uncertainties and variations of interpretation currently complained of would not be removed.

Finally, defining rate adequacy in terms of company solvency would restrict the ability of the states to achieve the other objectives of rate regulation. If rates were held to be insufficient only when they threatened the user's solvency, they would not be too low if they merely endangered rating bureaus or gave a company an unfair advantage in securing the best risks. A large multiple-line company apparently would be free to pursue such objectives by, for instance, under-pricing bodily injury liability coverage uniformly (so as to evade the unfair discrimination standard) so long as its solvency were not threatened.

Company Profits—The states whose laws now relate rate adequacy to company profits do so in terms of past or current profits. In Rhode Island, if the insurer can show that it is writing the particular kind of insurance at a profit "such showing shall be prima facie evidence that the rate or premium used is not inadequate."[75] This definition apparently would not apply to those filings involving new or modified forms of coverage. Also, it fails to state when rates *shall be* deemed inadequate.

The Minnesota definition says that rates are not inadequate if "the business being written at the rate proposed in the filing is being written by the insurer at a profit."[76] Since this relates only to current rates, it is not relevant to filings for rate reductions nor for new forms of coverage, although such filings are the ones most frequently in dispute.

Adequacy is related to company profit also in the bills recently proposed by Senator Kefauver for the District of Columbia, and by the National Association of Independent Insurers. These bills state that:

[75] Carlson, Thomas O., *op. cit.*, p. 58.
[76] *Ibid.*

No rate shall be held to be inadequate which upon reasonable assumptions of prospective loss and expense experience will not produce an underwriting loss.[77]

This statement has the merit of being a more concise and objective guide to the determination of rate adequacy; it focuses upon considerations intrinsic to the rate itself, equating adequacy with expected underwriting experience rather than with estimations of the probable effect upon solvency or competition.

In common with the Rhode Island definition previously cited, it has the short-coming of being stated in negative terms. It therefore limits the finding of inadequacy to instances when the filed rates would be reasonably expected to produce underwriting losses and precludes the regulatory authorities from disapproving rate reductions on other grounds. For example, disapprovals based upon the belief that certain minor rate reductions represented simply a superfluous addition to product heterogeneity would be barred.

In addition, stating the phrase in negative terms does not *require* disapproval of rates likely to produce an underwriting loss in spite of the fact that one of the stated objectives is to prevent loss-leaders[78] or market creaming.[79] If the phrase were stated in positive terms,[80] it would preclude this type of unfair pricing.

The fear has been expressed that this approach would bring about chaotic conditions and perhaps price warfare.[81] There is no reason why this should be the case. The practice to be guarded against is cutting rates below expected costs. As long as this is not done, price competition is not unfair, will not provoke a destructive rate war, and will not threaten the solvency of the low-rate insurer. On the contrary, this test of rate adequacy requires (if stated in positive terms) the regulatory officials to prevent any powerful company from bringing its superior financial resources to bear unfairly against its smaller rivals.

[77] *The National Underwriter,* September 9, 1960, p. 22.

[78] "Its purpose is to prevent a company from deliberately selling at rates expected to result in a loss. This will preclude loss-leaders." Letter from Vestal Lemmon, General Manager, National Association of Independent Insurers, Chicago, Illinois, June 28, 1960.

[79] The latter term is more descriptive of the practice of securing the above-average or "cream" risks by unfair pricing. Loss leadership generally refers to the retail marketing of certain items at a loss in order to induce customers to enter the store where, it is hoped, they will also buy other items.

[80] "Rates shall be held to be inadequate which upon reasonable assumptions of prospective loss and expense experience will produce an underwriting loss."

[81] *E.g., The National Underwrtier,* November 25, 1960, p. 12.

It is concluded that defining inadequate rates as those which would produce an underwriting loss would be a more clear and workable guide to the problems of insurer insolvency and unfair pricing than the other definitions which have been considered. Addition of this definition to the laws which now include no test of rate inadequacy would clarify the objectives of public control and simplify the administration of the insurance laws.

Two problems remain. The first is the possible need for public control of price competition in order to preserve the rating-bureau system. In the previous chapter the belief of certain members of the industry that price competition was threatening to destroy joint rate making was related.[82] However other industry leaders, including some bureau representatives, feel that greater flexibility of the rate regulatory process will preserve joint rating by enabling bureau companies to compete more effectively without withdrawing from the bureau to file independently.[83] The present study has not delved deeply enough into this issue to warrant evaluation of the need to control price competition for this particular purpose.

The other remaining problem is that of excessive product differentiation. There is perhaps no way of effectively and legally formalizing a requirement that filings for new rates, forms and rating systems represent true product improvement rather than additional, non-functional heterogeneity. Much could probably be achieved, however, through informal suggestion and persuasion by regulatory officials. A preferable manner of restricting product differentiation would be the voluntary adoption of a policy of restraint by the industry.

[82] *Cf.* Chapter IV, section discussing unrestricted competition as threat to joint pricing.
[83] *The National Underwriter,* February 17, 1961, pp. 38–9; *Ibid.,* March 24, 1961, p. 2.

CHAPTER VI

ALTERNATIVES TO RATE REGULATION

Certain alternative approaches to the problem of controlling automobile insurance rate levels may be feasible. These include regulation of company reserves rather than rates, confinement of regulation to the control of pure premiums, and insurance of company solvency. One or more of these methods may be practicable, especially since it has been found that workable competition prevails in this market. Still other alternatives might be the adoption of a multi-bureau system or abandonment of rate regulation altogether.

RESERVE REGULATION

Since competition is an adequate barrier to excessive rates, the major concern of public control is with rate adequacy and company solvency. Relating the adequacy standard to company profits, as described in the previous chapter, would improve state supervision of company solvency. The criticism has been made, however, that the states "have placed the cart before the horse by laying so much stress on rate supervision that regulation for solvency has become almost a forgotten art."[1]

It has been suggested that reserve regulation be strengthened where necessary and that reserves be relied upon to safeguard solvency, the companies being freed from the restraints of rate regulation. The proposal is based upon the belief that supervision of rate adequacy is an ineffectual means of protecting the interest of policyholders and claimants. This opinion was expressed by Kulp:

> The chief objective of state regulation of insurers is the safeguarding of their solvency; the chief device the state relies on to achieve this objective (backed by regulation of investments) is the requirement of minimum reserves. There are . . . other ways to protect insurer solvency, but even

[1] Kenney, Roger, "The Significance of Lloyd's Testimony Before the Senate Subcommittee," *United States Investor*, July 11, 1960, p. 57.

when they are applied, as in rate laws, they are essentially of secondary importance. Reserve regulation, as a matter of fact, provides a better check on rates than rate regulation on reserves. After all, the primary interest of the state is not so much that the proper amounts come into the insurer coffers as that when the day for paying claims arrives the proper amounts will be on hand.[2]

Out of concern with company solvency, the fact is often overlooked that there is no need for an insurance company to be kept in operation irrespective of the absence of any economic justification for its existence. "It is no worse for an ill-managed insurance company to have to cease underwriting than for any other business enterprise to have to close its doors,"[3] assuming that the company has enough assets to cover its policy obligations.

In England, where there is no governmental insurance rate regulation, solvency control takes the form of a required margin between assets and liabilities. Company assets must exceed liabilities by either fifty thousand pounds sterling or 10 per cent of the net premium income for the preceding year, whichever is greater. This provision is held to constitute "operational solvency rather than balance sheet solvency" and furnish protection against public injury through company failure.[4]

Automobile liability insurers in this country are required to maintain unearned premium reserves and loss reserves for the payment of claims on current and expired policies. The unearned premium reserve represents the portion of gross premiums on policies in force corresponding to their unexpired period. The loss reserve requirement is based upon the assumption that the average period needed to liquidate the losses will be 3 years and that the minimum cost to the company, including adjustment expense, will be 60 per cent of the premium. Thus the loss reserves must be 60 per cent of the premiums earned during the three previous policy years minus loss payments actually made, or the company's estimate of individual unsettled claims, whichever is higher.

If these reserves and others could be relied upon to protect insurer solvency, the states would be in a position to consider dis-

---

[2] Kulp, C. A., *Casualty Insurance*, p. 589.
[3] Brook, Herbert C., *op. cit.*, p. 621.
[4] Kadyk, David J., "Control and Regulation of British Insurance Companies," *Proceedings of the Section of Insurance Law*, American Bar Association, September 1950, p. 75.

pensing with rate regulation. They might be able to rely upon reserve regulation and competition to prohibit the use of rates that were too low or too high respectively. This is currently done in the field of life insurance.

But it does not appear to be possible to place this degree of reliance upon liability reserves. For one reason, underwriting experience is too volatile in this field (in contrast to life insurance) and too large an element of judgment is involved in determining the proper size of the loss reserves. A leading analyst of insurer finances, Roger Kenney, remarks that statutory reserve protection is "all to the good," and adds:

> But it still leaves open the question of the efficiency with which underwriting operations are conducted. A company which does not select its risks with care may well have an ultimate loss ratio in excess of the statutory standard of 60 cent. . . . Unless it sets up its loss reserves on a higher case basis—adequate to cover the higher incurred losses sustained—it is more than likely to be heading for trouble. In other words, the gap between the statutory standard and the actual loss reserves must be closed if the company is to remain in sound position. So, you see, you cannot legislate a casualty company into solvency or into good underwriting practice.[5]

Furthermore, the judgment of insurance executives is not unlikely to be affected by the desire to show favorable underwriting results in the annual statements. And the more conservative management is in reckoning future losses, the more difficult it is to show an underwriting profit, for estimated unpaid losses (as well as paid losses and expenses) are deducted from earned premiums in calculating underwriting profit or loss.[6]

The unearned premium reserve, as presently constituted, also has shortcomings as a means of protecting company solvency. This was pointed out by Professor Hedges:

> Finding a solution to the rate regulatory problem hinges upon coming up with a way to measure fire and casualty insurers' financial standing without reference to a rate level. Until this is done, anyone concerned with insuring the solvency of these companies must be directly concerned with where the rate level is. For present standards of solvency have this most peculiar characteristic: the lower the rate which a nonlife company charges for its insurance (and, therefore, presumably the thinner it is cutting its

[5] Kenney, Roger, *Fundamentals of Fire and Casualty Insurance Strength* (Dedham, Mass.: By the author, 1949), p. 192.

[6] *Ibid.*, pp. 182–3.

financial cushions), the fewer the assets which are required to establish its financial solvency.

This odd, not to say weird, relationship is due, of course, to the nature and use of the unearned premium reserve.[7]

The fact that the size of the current statutory reserves varies inversely with rate levels is an additional factor apparently prohibiting the substitution of reserve requirements for rate regulations. Perhaps research will some day develop better measures of future insurer liabilities so that solvency can be directly controlled while companies are left free to use whatever rates they wish. But at the present time, in Professor Hedges' words, "we just plain don't know enough about that variable which . . . is the basis on which we should regulate: the financial integrity of the companies."[8]

INSURANCE OF COMPANY SOLVENCY

Another possible method of securing the benefits of competition in automobile insurance while minimizing the public injury which might ensue would be the formal insuring of company solvency. The intent of this scheme would be to permit competitive pressures and managerial inadequacies to take their toll in the form of company failures, but to minimize the consequences of such failures. It would simply be an application of the insurance principles to the business of insurance itself.

Several plans of this nature are already in force on either an informal basis or in limited scale. The member underwriters at Lloyds of London contribute to a Central Guarantee Fund which would be available should a member be unable to meet his liabilities through other means.[9] Among British insurance companies there is an unwritten mutual assistance pact, a policy of providing voluntary support to any company that needs it.[10] Similar rescue operations have been performed from time to time by American companies out of "an awareness by well-managed companies that they would be hurt by the collapse of a poorly managed one, and rec-

[7] Statement of Bob A. Hedges, *Insurance Hearings*, p. 1111.
[8] *Ibid.*, p. 1084.
[9] Bohlinger, Alfred J., and Morrill, Thomas C., *op. cit.*, p. 55.
[10] *Ibid.*, p. 73.

ognition of the public relations value of preventing losses to policy-holders."[11]

In New York, a Life Insurance Guarantee Corporation has been established for the purpose of insuring payment of death claims under policies of insolvent life companies. As they are needed, funds can be assessed against all domestic life insurers up to a maximum of $25 million.[12]

New York and four other states (New Jersey, North Carolina, Pennsylvania and Wisconsin) have created Workmen's Compensation security funds to guarantee the payment of compensation claims by insolvent insurers. In each state the fund is financed by contributions of one per cent of the compensation premiums earned by companies writing the coverage in the state.[13]

Similar funds have been established by New York and New Jersey to protect policyholders and claimants of defunct automobile insurance companies. Insurers pay one per cent of written premiums in New York and half that amount in New Jersey to finance these plans until the funds reach a stipulated size.[14] In addition to paying claims on behalf of insolvent insurers, this scheme provides legal liability defense to those insureds whose companies are no longer in a position to provide this service.[15]

State funds like the New York and New Jersey Motor Vehicle Liability Security Funds are subject to the criticisms that they involve an uneconomical overlapping of reserves and expenses and bothersome duplications of administrative requirements.[16] Proposals have been made that the federal government establish a national insurance guarantee fund along the lines of the Federal Deposit Insurance Corporation,[17] or that the National Association of Insur-

---

[11] *The National Underwriter*, December 16, 1960, p. 8.

[12] National Association of Insurance Companies, *Proceedings*, 1952, p. 756.

[13] *Ibid.*, pp. 755–6.

[14] *Ibid.*, pp. 757–9.

[15] Bennett, Alfred C., *op. cit.*, pp. 16–17.

[16] Kenney, Roger, "American Mutual Insurance Alliance Takes Step to Preserve Private Enterprise," *United States Investor*, February 13, 1961, pp. 26–30.

[17] Heins, Richard M., "Liquidations of Insurance Companies," *Insurance and Government* (University of Wisconsin Insurance Series, Vol. II, No. 3; Madison; Fund for Insurance Education and Research, 1960), pp. 61–72.

ance Commissioners urge that uniform funds be set up by each of the states.[18]

The indications are that, if pushed very hard, either of the latter plans would meet with considerable opposition from the industry. The following criticisms were made when North Carolina was considering the creation of an automobile insolvency fund:

1. There is no need for such a fund; this is indicated by the fact that only two states now have them.
2. Insolvency funds tie up huge sums of money for long periods.
3. Unnecessary costs would be imposed upon policyholders, who ultimately must finance the funds.
4. Adequate supervision would prevent insolvency.
5. Poor management practices would be encouraged.[19]

Several of these objections relate to the very nature of insurance and might be used (though not by the same persons) to dissuade a prospective policyholder from buying, for example, a fire or theft policy.

A more substantial criticism of at least a federal program is that an additional structure of governmental regulation would be superimposed upon the ones that now exist in each of the 50 states. This has been the case with the Federal Deposit Insurance Corporation and has at times led to diffusion of authority and conflicts in supervisory policies.[20]

A federal program would also meet the opposition of many in the insurance industry who would oppose further intrusion by the federal government into their affairs. Many state officials would be likely to have a similar reaction.

Insurance of automobile claim payment by the state governments would also involve problems. The strength of the guarantee offered by 50 separate states would be much less than that of a single, unified fund. Before the Federal Deposit Insurance Corpora-

[18] In 1953 a N.A.I.C. subcommittee recommended "that the Association endorse the principle of security fund legislation in the areas of Workmen's Compensation Insurance and Automobile Liability Insurance." The recommendation was deleted before the subcommittee's report was received by the parent committee. National Association of Insurance Commissioners, *Proceedings, 1953,* pp. 593 and 601.

[19] These objections were raised by an official of the Association of Casualty and Surety Companies. Kenney, Roger, "American Mutual Insurance Alliance Takes Step to Preserve Private Enterprise," p. 26.

[20] See Bach, G. L., *Federal Reserve Policy Making* (New York: Alfred A. Knopf, 1950), Chaps. 6 and 10; Warburton, Clark, "Coordination of Monetary, Bank Supervisory, and Loan Agencies of the Federal Government," *Journal of Finance,* Vol. V, No. 2 (June 1950).

tion was created, 8 states had bank guarantee funds. Each of the 8 failed.[21]

In addition, there would be the problem of inducing the states to provide the insurance and to establish plans with similar strength and uniform provisions. The National Association of Insurance Commissioners could draw up a model plan and urge that it be adopted, but the decision would have to be made by each individual state. At this time there is no indication that the states would be willing to take action; they almost certainly would not in face of unified industry opposition.

In spite of these criticisms and difficulties, it does not seem that this proposal should be abandoned. People who believe in insurance and have made it their profession should be able to adapt it to eliminate the greatest risk of their own business. If this were done, price competition in automobile insurance could to a larger degree be freed from the restraints of public control, and the security of the protection offered by the industry would be greatly enhanced.

REGULATION OF PURE PREMIUMS

The pure premium is that part of the premium received which is needed by the company for the payment of losses. The recommendation is sometimes made that rate regulation and joint rating be confined to the pure premium and that free competition be permitted on the other parts of the premium dollar.

This proposal was brought forth by the counsel of the Senate Subcommittee investigating the insurance industry.[22] It was also made by the Attorney General of the United States in his brief in South-Eastern Underwriters Association case,[23] and was offered by an Assistant Attorney General in 1946:

> The need for combining the experience of all companies for rate purposes is reasonably clear. Insurance rates are founded upon the assumption that the future will, within reasonable limits, repeat the past. Accuracy of prediction, therefore, requires the broadest possible record of past performances. The experience of one or even a few companies may not be an adequate guide. But we must not forget that other factors enter a rate in

21 Heins, Richard M., op. cit., p. 62.
22 McHugh, Donald P., "The Role of Competition in Insurance Rate Making," Journal of the Bar Association of the District of Columbia, Vol. XXVI, No. 5, May 1959, p. 180.
23 Dineen, Robert E., "The A.I.C. Bills and their Alternatives," p. 31.

addition to what might be termed "pure cost" based upon past experience. Any final rate also includes administrative expense, acquisition cost and profit. These are not uniform for all companies. Any rate agreed upon by competitors must be so weighted as to protect the least efficient operator. Thus the necessity for using common experience in reaching an individual judgment on rates will not justify agreement upon the same final rate by all companies.

The need to make use of common experience or even to use a basic rate floor derived from such experience does not necessitate depriving the public of the benefits of competition.[24]

Thus this scheme would contemplate joint determination of the pure premium, but competition on each other element of the total premium.

The plan is beguilingly simple and deceptively logical. Its principal shortcoming is that even the pure premium data of all companies are not homogeneous because of the use of different classification plans, territorial definitions and policy coverages. "The experience of one company in such a situation is just not comparable on any terms with the experience of another company and the combined result is accordingly meaningless from an actuarial standpoint."[25] In order to be made workable this system would in some respects have to be less flexible than the All-Industry approach, since the latter permits inter-company differences in rating systems, territories, and coverages.

Other criticisms of pure premium regulation include the following:

1. The expense experience of small companies often lacks statistical credibility.
2. Insurance departments would have the problem of examining a vast number of different rates.
3. Many smaller companies are not equipped to prepare rate filings and their supporting information.
4. Since each company has a different expense ratio, the problem of rate diversity would be magnified.[26]

As Carlson commented, "It is unfortunate that an apparent plausibility not supported by scientific consideration lends enchant-

[24] Berge, Wendell, "Insurance and the Antitrust Laws," *Proceedings of the Section of Insurance Law,* American Bar Association, October 1946, p. 33.

[25] Carlson, Thomas O., *op. cit.,* p. 52.

[26] Testimony of Commissioner Knowlton of New Hampshire, former President of the National Association of Insurance Commissioners, *Insurance Hearings,* pp. 1842–3.

ment to this particular prospect and yet the consideration which should be precedent to such a combination of experience, that is, complete uniformity in class, territory and coverage definitions, is repugnant *per se* because it would stifle experimental and competitive developments which furnish life-blood to the industry."[27]

MULTI-BUREAU SYSTEM

A fourth alternative to present practices might be a system featuring mandatory membership of all automobile insurers in any one of several rating bureaus. This is suggested not so much as a currently practical solution to the problems of public control as an illustration of one system which would alleviate many of these problems. The multi-bureau system would be a compromise solution intended to strike a workable balance between public protection and free enterprise, between price uniformity and competition.

There might, for instance, be 3 rating bureaus. Each insurer would have to belong to 1 of the 3 and use the rates, forms and rating systems promulgated by that particular bureau on the basis of the pooled experience of its members. Each company would be free to choose whichever of the bureaus it wished to join and could transfer to 1 of the other 2 at any time it wished. Rates promulgated by each bureau would be subject to state approval or disapproval as at present.

In view of the industry's present composition, the line-up of the 3 rating organizations (if this were the number authorized) might, at least originally, be something on this order: (1) Bureau A—members of the present national bureaus, (2) Bureau B—primarily the smaller companies which now use the American agency system and deviate a fixed percentage from bureau rates, and (3) Bureau C—the currently independent, low-rate direct writing companies.

Since all carriers would belong to a bureau and use rates based upon pooled statistics, survival of the joint pricing system would be guaranteed. With it, the stability and reliability of rate levels would be assured.

The number of different rates, rating systems, and policy forms would be limited to three. Diminution of the number of filings

[27] Carlson, Thomas O., *loc. cit.*

would greatly facilitate state regulation. Regulators would be in a much better position to prevent rate and commission wars, market creaming maneuvers, and quality reduction.

What about competition? One cannot say with certainty what the results of such an industry structure would be, but it is entirely possible that rivalry among the three groups would be even more effective than is competition among the more than 600 firms now in the automobile insurance business.

Since the number of alternatives open to consumers would be, in some respects,[28] limited to three, proponents of the competing groups would be better able to educate the public as to the merits of their own product, and consumers would be in a much better position to make rational purchase decisions. Because of this, each bureau would have considerable incentive to adopt price reductions and product innovations attractive to policy buyers. Also, the price and policy modifications adopted would be subject to the verdict of a better informed public, a fact which might very well justify a more liberal attitude on the part of certain regulatory officials.

Whitney concludes his two volume work on anti-trust policy with the following statement:

> The pure competition of small firms, each producing as much as it can at a cost below the prevailing market price, and meeting that price, would not be dynamic or progressive. In fact, it could "hardly be called competitive at all." While monopolies have been shown to possess grave defects . . . the *hope* of winning profits which certain kinds of monopolistic position provide is a driving force for both business firm and individual without which our economy might well stagnate. The firm or individual may seek a profitable patent, the success that comes from making the most popular product, or the extra reward of special skill and efficiency; both are inspired to their efforts by something far different from the hope of earning a "normal return" under pure competition.[29]

History indicates that public control of the automobile business will not remain unchanged. It is likely to become either more permissive or more restrictive. Adoption of some of the features of a multi-bureau system would be a way to preserve the merits of private enterprise and at the same time achieve the objectives which otherwise may be sought through tightened governmental control.

---

[28] Individual firms would still compete on the basis of service, financial condition, country-wide claim representatives, availability of other lines and so forth.
[29] Whitney, Simon N., *op. cit.*, p. 438.

ABANDONMENT OF REGULATION

A final alternative might be the discontinuance of efforts to limit price competition in this industry. This would be a simple way to resolve what appears to be a growing conflict between the antitrust approach favored by some federal officials and the traditional method of state regulated price competition.[30]

Abandonment of rate regulation would hasten the attrition of the smaller and weaker companies which is already under way.[31] Even under present conditions many people feel that only the largest and strongest automobile insurers may survive the next few decades.[32] Some estimate that as few as 10 or 20 per cent of the companies will remain 20 years from now.[33] Thus, if government withdrew from rate regulation the result in a comparatively short time would likely be an oligopolistic industry which would have many of the merits of the multi-bureau system just described.

It has been remarked that price regulation of casualty insurance "does not seem to be very practical, or particularly satisfactory to anybody."[34] Why not, then, give up rate regulation and simply do as Whitney suggests:

> Let those insurers who wish to write their rates in common be allowed to do so, just so long as others . . . are permitted to file independent rates. Among the great number of insurance companies, some can then be counted on to introduce enough competition into the total structure to prevent monopolistic exploitation of the policyholders.[35]

The trouble with this approach is that "monopolistic exploitation of the policyholders" is not presently a problem. To concentrate upon it leads one to ignore matters which *are* current problems, namely (1) occasional company insolvency and the resultant injury to the public, (2) unfair pricing practices, (3) too much diversity of rates and forms, and (4) the possible threat to joint pricing. Be-

[30] Dineen, Robert E., Procter, Clifford R., and Gardner, H. Daniel, "The Economics and Principles of Insurance Supervision," *Insurance and Government* (University of Wisconsin Insurance Series, Vol. II, No. 1; Madison: Fund for Insurance Education and Research, 1960), p. 60.

[31] During the period 1953–57 there were 187 insurance company mergers. McHugh, Donald P., "Federal Investigation of Insurance," p. 6.

[32] *E.g.*, Cosgrove, John N., *op. cit.*, p. 259; Rennie, Robert A., *op. cit.*, p. 81.

[33] See Lang, Frank, "Operating Trends," *Best's Insurance News*, July 1960, p. 21.

[34] Force, Kenneth O., "Regulation is Asked for What It Can't Be Expected to Deliver," *The National Underwriter*, May 16, 1958, p. 27.

[35] Whitney, Simon N., *op. cit.*, p. 359.

cause competitive pressures are increasing, the first of these, particularly, would be aggravated if government were to leave pricing practices completely uncontrolled. All are of sufficient importance to justify governmental concern.

Regulation of automobile insurance rates can be improved. It also can be simplified and made more uniform. Greater reliance can be placed upon competition to prevent rate excessiveness. Rate adequacy can be judged with reference to the likelihood of future profits.

If reserve regulation were improved or if a system of insuring company solvency were developed, public control could properly be liberalized. Until this is done, or until a marked change in industry structure and performance occurs, public regulation of automobile insurance rates is necessary.

CHAPTER VII

SUMMARY AND CONCLUSION

The regulation of automobile insurance rates involves many contradictions, considerable uncertainty, and much dispute. This perhaps should be expected since "insurance is a competitive business, at least as much as it is a mathematical-social technique" and is no more logical and internally consistent than any other commercial institution.[1]

The contradictions of rate regulation are inherent in the laws which call for competition among insurance carriers and at the same time permit cooperative rate making. Much of the dispute arises from the fact that while almost everyone, whether supervisory official or company executive, believes strongly in the merits of competitive free enterprise, many of these same people see a need, for one purpose or another, to limit price competition in insurance. The uncertainty referred to is encountered by anyone who seeks to reconcile these conflicting points of view; it rests most heavily upon the shoulders of those insurance commissioners whose laws fail to define the nature of inadequate or excessive rates.

In order to facilitate the analysis, this study has concentrated upon one form of insurance, the automobile policy. It is felt, however, that the performance and problems of rate regulation in this sector of the industry are relevant to the entire subject of insurance supervision.

Many of the economic characteristics of the automobile insurance business are pertinent to the issues of its control. This is a relatively young business, the first policy having been issued in 1898. By 1960, however, over 73 million motor vehicles were registered in the United States, and premiums exceeded $6 billion.

The industry's product is an unusual one. The automobile policy is a complex legal document constituting a promise by the seller to

[1] Kulp, C. A., *op. cit.,* p. 484.

perform certain services for the buyer dependent upon future contingencies. In spite of the fact that most people cannot understand the contract and expect to receive no payment from the seller during its term, the great majority of those who own automobiles buy the coverage. The demand is relatively inelastic.

The supply of automobile insurance is highly elastic. Entry into the industry is rather easy. Fixed costs are low. While the optimum size of automobile insurers is unknown, there do not appear to be great economies of large-scale operation.

The insurance agent plays a strategic role because he, in a sense, produces the business. One of the most significant features of the business is the variation in agency systems. Intense competition exists between companies using the traditional American agency system and those which use the newer, so-called direct-writing system. This rivalry has been the source of much of the dynamic and progressive spirit which now dominates the business and has provided the incentive for many of the innovations which have occurred in recent years.

Concentration of economic power is not presently a problem in automobile insurance. Over 600 companies write the coverage and the 20 largest write less than 50 per cent of the annual premium. The two largest insurers, State Farm and Allstate, together write only 14 per cent of the total premium.

Several forms of nonprice competition prevail. Many companies appeal to prospective insurers on the basis of agency and claim service or similar inducements. The evidence indicates, however, that price competition is more significant. Price differentials among some companies probably average 20 per cent or more.

State governments for many years have attempted to supervise insurance pricing activities, but effective regulation is a recent development. During the 1880's American fire insurance companies developed the compact system, a method of jointly making and maintaining uniform rate levels. The reaction of many states was the adoption of anti-compact laws which attempted to apply the anti-trust principle of compulsory competition to insurance.

Experience proved the anti-compact approach to be unsatisfactory. The loss and expense experience of individual insurance companies, unless they are of great size, is not sufficient to serve as a reliable indicator of future probabilities and hence not adequate for the creation of reliable rates. Recognizing this, the states gradually repealed the anti-compact laws, replacing them with rate regulatory statutes. The latter permitted companies to pool their experience statistics and calculate uniform rates; the state insurance department was given the responsibility of supervising the rate-making bureaus and the rates which they promulgated.

State regulation of insurance rates received federal sanction in 1945 when Congress adopted a law exempting joint rate making activities from the anti-trust acts, provided that the states exercise effective regulation. In the years immediately following this action, most of the states enacted what are known as All-Industry rate regulatory laws. It is these laws which both permit cooperative pricing and encourage price competition.

The All-Industry laws also state that rates shall be neither excessive nor inadequate, but, generally, they do not define these two terms. Evaluation of rate filings is thus left to the individual commissioner. His actions will reflect his judgment of what rates are too high and what rates are too low. It is his judgment also which will determine the width of the range between excessiveness and inadequacy, or, in other words, the amount of price competition which is to be permitted.

There are many opinions as to how much price competition should be allowed in automobile insurance. In some states little or none is allowed, the regulatory authorities requiring either practical or absolute price uniformity. At the opposite extreme are those jurisdictions where little if any limitation is put upon price competition. Rate supervisors in most states attempt to achieve a compromise between the two extremes.

The issue of controlling price competition is a crucial one, as it involves a fundamental conflict between major industry forces. Resolution of the conflict will affect the fortunes of rival insurance companies. It will also affect the price and the security of the insurance made available to the public.

Those who favor stringent public control of price competition base their case upon the following contentions: (1) price competition is likely to drive rates down to inadequate levels, endangering company solvency, (2) joint pricing by rating bureaus is necessary for the determination of reliable rates, (3) price competition threatens the survival of the rating bureaus, (4) price competition may degenerate into commission wars, (5) price competition encourages quality reductions, (6) regulation is necessary to prevent unfair pricing practices, (7) competition produces excessive numbers of rates, rating systems, and policy forms.

Other persons maintain that considerable price competition is desirable and that automobile insurers should be free to establish their own rates within a broad range. This viewpoint is based upon the following contentions: (1) the ideals of free enterprise are appropriate to insurance and will give the public the benefit of low-cost protection, (2) determination of a proper uniform rate is not feasible because of differences among companies, (3) price and commission wars are highly unlikely, as is indicated by those instances where insurance rates are not regulated, (4) insurer insolvencies are caused by factors other than low rates and cannot be prevented by rate regulation, (5) restriction of price competition also imposes limits upon nonprice competition, (6) efforts to curtail price competition aggravate administrative problems, including political pressures and the burden of scrutinizing rate filings.

It was found that disagreement on the issue of controlling price competition is the fundamental cause of many of the disputes over rate regulation. Each person's position on this basic issue affects his judgment of the need for governmental control of rate excessiveness and rate adequacy.

The problems of rate regulation are clarified, however, if the two rate standards are considered separately. The study therefore analyzed the control of high rates and of low rates as individual subjects. In each instance, an attempt was made (1) to identify the goals of public control, (2) to evaluate the importance of these goals and the effectiveness of rate regulation as a means of achieving them, and (3) to determine the most appropriate manner of applying rate regulation for these purposes.

The purpose of controlling rate excessiveness is to prevent exploitation of the policy-buying public by the rating bureau system.

When the states abandoned the anti-compact approach and legalized joint rate making, regulation to prevent monopolistic pricing became necessary. This purpose is made explicit by the laws of several states which provide that rates shall not be deemed excessive if a reasonable degree of competition prevails.

The conclusion was reached that it is desirable to relate rate excessiveness to the lack of competition in the foregoing manner. Application of a selected set of tests led to the judgment that workable competition presently does exist in the automobile insurance market. This precludes abuse of the joint pricing privilege; maintenance of excessive rates is impossible under present conditions. So long as workable competition persists, stringent public control to prevent the use of excessive automobile insurance rates is unnecessary. Amendment of the insurance regulatory laws to define rate excessiveness in terms of competition would be in the public interest.

Regulation of rate adequacy is complicated by a diversity of purposes. Lack of agreement as to the intent of such regulation beclouds the issues and fosters dispute and uncertainty.

Controversy over administration of the adequacy standard has been further intensified by the price competition of direct-writing insurers. By offering and aggressively merchandising coverage at low rates, these companies have secured a great volume of business and have challenged many of the industry's traditional patterns and practices.

There are four possible major objectives of controlling rate adequacy. These are (1) prevention of rate wars and company insolvency, (2) avoidance of unfair pricing practices, (3) preservation of the joint pricing system, and (4) restriction of product differentiation.

The first of the four goals, prevention of rate wars and company insolvency, is generally regarded as the most vital. There appear to be strong theoretical grounds for believing that unrestrained price competition would be likely to force rates below the level of adequacy. However, the actual record of insurer insolvencies and the absence of rate wars, even in those instances where rates are not controlled, tend to discredit the supposition that price competition is apt to cause company failures. The available evidence, although meager, indicates that the insolvencies which have occurred are not attributable to the use of low rates. It was concluded that, while government must be able to restrict price competition for the purpose of protecting insurer solvency, the need for such control has been exaggerated. The insurance laws could properly be amended to clarify and simplify this objective.

The second possible objective of controlling rate adequacy is to prevent the use of unfair pricing practices. It has been alleged that certain companies have secured automobile business by writing it at prices below cost and later either have raised the rates or have gotten rid of all but the above-average risks. It was concluded that the rate regulatory laws should be amended to clarify this objective and prohibit such practices.

The control of price competition as a means of preserving the joint pricing system is urged by some industry leaders. Other persons feel either that the rating bureaus are not essential or that they do not need protection from competitive pressures. This is an important issue and one which deserves thorough and impartial research. The present study has set forth many of the points which are relevant to this issue and has demonstrated the need to treat it as but one of several possible goals of public control. The study has not, however, attempted to make the intensive analysis of the joint pricing system which would warrant an evaluation of the need to control price competition for this particular purpose.

Finally, rate adequacy might be regulated for the purpose of restricting product differentiation. There currently exists in automobile insurance an excessive number of rates, rating systems, and policy forms. Enforcement of a reasonable degree of standardization would facilitate the analysis of alternative purchases by consumers. The efforts of state regulation to compel insurers to follow those practices which are in the public interest would then be supplemented by the pressure of a better informed consumer demand.

The laws of several states include definitions or tests of rate inadequacy. These relate inadequate rates to (1) destruction of competition, (2) threats to company solvency, or (3) underwriting losses. The first two of these approaches were deemed to be inferior to the last. It was concluded that defining inadequate rates as those which would produce an underwriting loss would facilitate regulation for the purposes of (1) preventing rate wars and insurer insolvencies, and (2) avoiding the use of unfair pricing practices. Inclusion of this definition in the statutes which now contain no test of rate inadequacy would clarify the objectives of public control and simplify its administration.

None of the current or proposed definitions of adequacy is designed to deal with the problem of the possible threat to joint rate making. It would perhaps be impossible to secure enough agreement at this time to make such a statement workable; dispute over the issue is probably too intense. As previously indicated, however, study of the role of rating bureaus and of the implications for regulatory policies is needed.

The definition suggested above would not help to implement the fourth objective of controlling rate adequacy, the restriction of nonfunctional product heterogeneity. For this purpose, informal persuasion by state officials and the exercise of restraint by insurers would probably be more suitable than the use of the formal rate-regulatory machinery.

The study reviewed several alternative approaches to the control of automobile insurance rates. The first, substitution of reserve regulation for rate regulation, is not feasible due to shortcomings in the nature of present reserve requirements. Future research may develop better measures of prospective company liabilities, enabling solvency to be controlled directly rather than through supervision of rate adequacy.

A second alternative approach to the control of solvency would be the establishment of a system to insure policyholders and claimants against loss resulting from company failure. The problems associated with this approach appear to be chiefly political rather than inherent defects of the plan. The proposal deserves serious study.

The third alternative considered was that rate regulation be confined to pure premiums, the portion of the rate needed for loss payments. This was rejected on the grounds that, because of differences in rating systems, territorial definitions, and policy coverages, the pure premium data of all companies are not homogeneous. The data could be made comparable only by imposing stringent restrictions upon inter-company differences.

A fourth alternative was presented in the form of a multi-bureau system. Mandatory membership of all automobile insurers in any one of several rating bureaus would be a way of solving many of the current problems of public control. It would guarantee survival of the joint pricing system and the advantages associated with that system. It would reduce the variety of rates, rating systems, and policy forms to the authorized number of competing bureaus. This reduction would facilitate state regulation and greatly enhance the ability of consumers to choose their automobile coverage rationally. A multi-bureau system would be a means of achieving the major objectives of insurance regulation with a minimum of governmental control of insurance company operations.

Finally, the abandonment of automobile insurance rate regulation was considered. While it is true that present regulatory practices do not completely satisfy anyone, public interest in the provision of sound insurance protection at reasonable prices is too great to justify abandoning regulation.

Regulation can be improved. It can be simplified and made more uniform. It also can be made less uncertain in its aims and its application. Adoption of statutory definitions of inadequate and excessive rates would be a valuable step in this direction.

Adoption of the suggested definitions would permit a reduction in the amount of detailed supervision of routine rate filings. It is felt that this would not reduce, but probably would increase, the effectiveness of rate regulation. The definitions would focus attention upon the specific purposes of public control and would establish the principle that so long as competition is reasonable (*i.e.*, not outside the zone prescribed by the definitions), it is in the public interest. To the extent that regulatory procedures could then be simplified, supervisory officials would be better able to concentrate upon more important matters, including the relatively few instances of actually excessive or inadequate rates.

During future years, rate regulation will be faced with "stupendous problems arising by virtue of highly competitive forces meeting head-on in the arena of the insurance market."[2] In order to handle these problems successfully officials of both government and industry will need to approach them with as objective an attitude as possible. The need for a particular type of control for one specific purpose (such as controlling rate adequacy to prevent unfair discrimination) should not be assumed to justify other forms of regulation for other purposes. Likewise, the need for control over one part of the insurance industry (such as automobile insurance) should not be taken as justification for unnecessarily broad controls over other areas of the industry. Rather, the specific purposes of public control should be identified, and each regulatory problem considered in relation to the competitive patterns and practices in the particular insurance market which is involved. Furthermore, it must be recognized that as insurance practices are modified and as competitive forces are realigned, regulatory practices and policies must also be modified.

Insurance regulation perhaps never can avoid controversy. There is an innate conflict between the interests of the regulator and the regulated, and an inherent contradiction in the public *control* of price *competition*. The most satisfactory balance between control and competition must be sought. The probability of achieving this balance will be increased if those seeking it make an effort to identify and clarify the objectives of insurance regulation, and if they continuously bear in mind that it is the public interest which must be served.

[2] Gerber, Joseph S., *op. cit.*, p. 92.

BIBLIOGRAPHY

Public Documents

The Attorney General's National Committee to Study the Antitrust Laws. *Report.* Washington: U.S. Government Printing Office, 1955.

U.S. Senate, Subcommittee on Anti-trust and Monopoly of the Committee on the Judiciary. *Hearings on the Insurance Industry.* 85th Congress and 86th Congress, 1958, 1959, 1960.

————. *The Insurance Industry: Aviation, Ocean Marine, and State Regulation.* Report No. 1834, 86th Congress, 2nd Session, 1960.

————. *The Insurance Industry: Insurance: Rates, Rating Organizations, and State Rate Regulation.* Report No. 831, 87th Congress, 1st Session, 1961.

Books

BACKMAN, JULES. *Surety Rate-Making.* New York: The Surety Association of America, 1948.

Best's Fire and Casualty Aggregates and Averages. New York: Alfred M. Best Co., annual.

Best's Insurance Reports (Fire and Casualty). New York: Alfred M. Best Co., annual.

BICKLEY, JOHN S. *Trends and Problems in the Distribution of Property-Liability Insurance.* (Research Monograph No. R-91.) Columbus: Bureau of Business Research, Ohio State University, 1956.

BOHLINGER, ALFRED J., AND MORRILL, THOMAS C. *Insurance Supervision and Practices in England.* New York: State of New York Insurance Department, 1948.

COSGROVE, JOHN N. *Competition in Insurance Marketing.* Cincinnati: National Underwriter Co., 1960.

Council of State Governments, Insurance Committee. *Revision of State Systems for Insurance Regulation.* Chicago: Council of State Governments, 1946.

COWEE, JOHN W., AND CENTER, CHARLES C. *Federal Regulation of Insurance.* (Wisconsin Commerce Reports, Vol. II, No. 3.) Madison: University of Wisconsin, School of Commerce, Bureau of Business Research and Service, 1949.

HAMILTON, WALTON. *Politics in Industry.* New York: Alfred A. Knopf, 1957.

HEDGES, J. EDWARD, AND McMASTERS, CLYDE V. *The Effects of Public Law Fifteen on the Local Insurance Agent.* (Indiana Business Studies, No. 34.) Bloomington: Bureau of Business Research, Indiana University, 1952.

Insurance Industry Committee, *In the Public Interest: One Hundred Years of Insurance Supervision in New York State.* New York: Insurance Industry Committee for the New York Insurance Department Centennial, 1960.

KENNEY, ROGER. *Fundamentals of Fire and Casualty Insurance Strength*. Dedham, Massachusetts. By the author, 1949.

KIMBALL, SPENCER L. *Insurance and Public Policy*. Madison: University of Wisconsin Press, 1960.

KULP, C. A. *Casualty Insurance*. 3rd ed. New York: Ronald Press, 1956.

National Association of Insurance Commissioners. *Proceedings*, annual.

PATTERSON, EDWIN W. *The Insurance Commissioner in the United States*. Cambridge: Harvard University Press, 1927.

SAWYER, ELMER W. *Insurance as Interstate Commerce*. New York: McGraw-Hill, 1945.

WANDEL, WILLIAM HAMLIN. *The Control of Competition in Fire Insurance*. Lancaster, Pa.: By the author, 1935.

WHITNEY, SIMON N. *Antitrust Policies*. Vol. II. New York: Twentieth Century Fund, 1958.

WILLIAMS, C. ARTHUR. *Price Discrimination in Property and Liability Insurance*. (University of Minnesota Studies in Economics and Business, No. 19.) Minneapolis: University of Minnesota Press, 1959.

ZOFFER, H. JEROME. *The History of Automobile Liability Insurance Rating*. Pittsburgh: University of Pittsburgh Press, 1959.

Articles and Periodicals

BELCHER, FRANK B. "Insurance Rate Regulation and Free Enterprise," *Proceedings of the Section of Insurance Law*, American Bar Association, September 1947, pp. 23–28.

BELL, S. ALEXANDER. "Competition," *Best's Insurance News*, October 1954, pp. 29–32.

————. "Independent's Experience," *Best's Insurance News*, June 1960, pp. 107–111.

BENNETT, ALFRED C. "Liquidations of Insurance Companies," *Insurance and Government*. (University of Wisconsin Insurance Series, Vol. II, No. 3.) Madison: Fund for Insurance Education and Research, 1960, pp. 1–40.

BERGE, WENDELL. "Insurance and the Anti-Trust Laws," *Proceedings of the Section of Insurance Law*, American Bar Association, October 1946, pp. 29–34.

BERGSON, HERBERT A. "Regulation *v.* Competition," *Insurance Law Journal*, No. 406, November 1956, pp. 703–708.

BLANCHARD, RALPH H. "Judgment Helps Set Our Rates," *The Spectator*, August 1953, pp. 14 ff.

BROOK, HERBERT C. "Public Interest and the Commissioners'-All-Industry Laws," *Law and Contemporary Problems*, XV, No. 4, Autumn 1950, pp. 606–629.

BRUNDAGE, JOHN D. "The Urge to Merge," *Best's Insurance News*, December 1959, pp. 94 ff.

CARLSON, THOMAS O. "Rate Regulation and the Casualty Actuary," *Proceedings of the Casualty Actuarial Society*, Vol. XXXVIII, No. 69, May 1951, pp. 9–72.

CAVERLY, RAYMOND N. "The Background of the Casualty and Bonding Business in the United States," *Insurance Counsel Journal,* VI, No. 4, October 1939, pp. 62–67.

CLARK, J. M., "Toward a Concept of Workable Competition," *American Economic Review,* Vol. XXX, No. 2, June, 1940.

COLLINS, JOSEPH F. "Rate Regulation in Fire and Casualty Insurance," *Examination of Insurance Companies.* Vol. V. New York: New York State Insurance Department, 1955, pp. xv–xliii.

DINEEN, ROBERT E. "The AIC Bills and the Alternatives," *Journal of American Insurance,* XXIII, November 1946, pp. 27–32.

————. "The Regulator's Viewpoint," *The Implications of Federal Control Over Insurance* (Insurance Series, No. 66.) New York: American Management Association, 1946, pp. 3–11.

DINEEN, ROBERT E.; PROCTER, CLIFFORD R.; AND GARDNER, H. DANIEL. "The Economics and Principles of Insurance Supervision," *Insurance and Government.* (University of Wisconsin Insurance Series, Vol. II, No. 1.) Madison: Fund for Insurance Education and Research, 1960, pp. 1–78.

DIRLAM, JOEL B., AND STELZER, IRWIN M. "The Insurance Industry: A Case Study in the Workability of Regulated Competition," *University of Pennsylvania Law Review,* CVII, No. 2, December 1958, pp. 199–215.

DONOVAN, JAMES B. "Insurance—The Case in Favor of Existing Exemptions from the Antitrust Laws," *Federal Bar Journal,* XX, No. 1, Winter 1960, pp. 56–65.

————. "Rate Regulations Revisited," *Insurance and Government.* (University of Wisconsin Insurance Series, Vol. II, No. 4.) Madison: Fund for Insurance Education and Research, 1960, pp. 1–26.

————. "Regulation of Insurance Under the McCarran Act," *Law and Contemporary Problems,* XV, No. 4, Autumn 1950, pp. 473–492.

DOWNEY, E. H. "The Public Supervision of Workmen's Compensation Insurance," *Modern Insurance Problems.* Philadelphia: The American Academy of Political and Social Science, 1917, pp. 297–316.

ELY, ROBERT B. "Governmental Regulation," *Best's Insurance News,* February 1954, pp. 33–41.

————. "Governmental Regulation of Insurance Marketing Practices," *Insurance Law Journal,* No. 374, March 1954, pp. 186–195.

EPES, W. PERRY. "Rate Regulation Revisited," *Insurance and Government.* (University of Wisconsin Insurance Series, Vol. II, No. 4.) Madison, Wisconsin: Fund for Insurance Education and Research, 1960, pp. 48–80.

EVANS, HAROLD G. "The Auto Insurance Dilemma," *Best's Insurance News,* January 1960, pp. 20 ff.

FORCE, KENNETH O. "Auto Is More Complex, Competitive," *The National Underwriter,* June 10, 1960, p. 42.

GERBER, JOSEPH S. "Rate Regulation Revisited: The Point of View of the States," *Insurance and Government* (University of Wisconsin Insurance Series, Vol. II, No. 4.) Madison, Wisconsin: Fund for Insurance Education and Research, 1960, pp. 81–94.

————. "Guide to Insurance Markets," *The Spectator*, November 1960, pp. 53–84.

HANSEN, VICTOR R. "Merger of Insurance Companies and Anti-trust Law," *Insurance Law Journal*, No. 431, December 1958, pp. 782–791.

HAVIGHURST, HAROLD C. "State *vs.* Federal Regulation of Insurance," *Journal of the American Association of University Teachers of Insurance*, VIII, No. 1, March 1941, pp. 57–67.

HEINS, RICHARD M. "Liquidations of Insurance Companies," *Insurance and Government*. (University of Wisconsin Insurance Series, Vol. II, No. 3.) Madison: Fund for Insurance Education and Research, 1960, pp. 41–72.

HOBBS, CLARENCE W. "State Regulation of Insurance Rates," *Proceedings of the Casualty Actuarial Society*, XI, No. 24, 1925, pp. 218–275.

————. "State Regulation of Insurance Rates," *Proceedings of the Casualty Actuarial Society*, XXVIII, No. 58, 1942, pp. 344–470.

JAMIESON, R. G. "Has Competition Made Present Rating Laws Obsolete?" *Insurance Law Journal*, No. 394, November 1955, pp. 721–722.

KADYK, DAVID J. "Control and Regulation of British Insurance Companies," *Proceedings of the Section of Insurance Law*, American Bar Association, September 1950, pp. 63–87.

KAHN, HARRY A. "Liability Insurance Rates: Automobile Liability," *Examination of Insurance Companies*, Vol. V, New York: New York State Insurance Department, 1955, pp. 69–84.

KENNEY, ROGER. "Bureaus Have Lost Their 'Paramount' Position in Fire and Casualty Business," *United States Investor*, August 1, 1960, pp. 21–25.

————. "Critique of American Agency System," *Readings in Property and Casualty Insurance*, ed., H. Wayne Snider. Homewood, Illinois: Richard D. Irwin, Inc., 1959.

————. "Rate Deviations Become Whipping Boy of Reactionaries in Insurance Industry," *United States Investor*, June 15, 1957, pp. 23–38.

KIMBALL, SPENCER L., AND BOYCE, RONALD N. "The Adequacy of State Insurance Rate Regulation: The McCarran-Ferguson Act in Historical Perspective," *Michigan Law Review*, LVI, No. 4, February 1958, pp. 545–578.

KIMBALL, SPENCER L., AND HANSEN, W. EUGENE. "The Utah Insurance Commissioner: A Study of Administrative Regulation in Action," *Utah Law Review*, V, No. 4, Fall, 1957, pp. 429–455.

KIMBALL, SPENCER L., AND JACKSON, BARTLETT A. "The Regulation of Insurance Marketing," *Columbia Law Review*, Vol. LXI, February 1961, pp. 141–200.

KLINE, GEORGE H. "Casualty Rates and Rating," *Insurance Counsel Journal*, XXVI, No. 1, January 1959, pp. 49–56.

KLITZKE, RAMON A. "Fire Insurance Rates and the Law," *Insurance Law Journal*, No. 405, October 1956, pp. 631–649.

KULP, C. A. "The Rate Making Process in Property and Casualty Insurance—Goals, Technics, and Limits," *Law and Contemporary Problems*, XV, No. 4, Autumn 1950, pp. 493–522.

LANG, FRANK. "Automobile Insurance Marketing," *Best's Insurance News*, June 1955, pp. 25 ff.

LEMMON, VESTAL. "The N.A.I.I." *Best's Insurance News*, December 1956, pp. 91 ff.

LITTLETON, OTIS. "The Marketing Concept, Its Application to Insurance and How It Can Improve the Competitive Position of the American Agency System," *The Annals of the Society of Chartered Property and Casualty Underwriters*, Vol. XII, No. 1, January 1960, pp. 56–57.

McHUGH, DONALD P. "Rate Regulation Revisited: The Point of View of a Federal Official," *Insurance and Government* (University of Wisconsin Insurance Series, Vol. II, No. 4.) Madison, Wisconsin: Fund for Insurance Education and Research, 1960, pp. 95–127.

————. "The Role of Competition in Insurance Rate Making," *Journal of the Bar Association of the District of Columbia*, XXVI, No. 5, May 1959, pp. 173–190.

MARRYOT, FRANKLIN J. "Mutual Insurance Under Rate Regulation," *Law and Contemporary Problems*, XV, No. 4, Autumn 1950, pp. 540–562.

————. "Rate Regulation Revisited," *Insurance and Government* (University of Wisconsin Insurance Series, Vol. II, No. 4.) Madison, Wisconsin: Fund for Insurance Education and Research, 1960, pp. 27–47.

————. "Twelve Years of Insurance as Commerce—Prospects for the Future," *Insurance Counsel Journal*, XXIII, No. 3, July 1957, pp. 191–197.

————. "Why Regulate Insurance Rates?" *Proceedings of the Section of Insurance Law*, American Bar Association, October 1946, pp. 305–317.

MARTIN, WADE O., JR., "The N.A.I.C. and State Insurance Department Functions," *Insurance Law Journal*, No. 356, September 1952 pp. 583–587.

MATTHIAS, RUSSELL H., AND ROBISON, CHARLES B. "State Regulation of Insurance Rates," *Insurance Law Journal*, No. 355, August 1952, pp. 537–542.

MERTZ, ARTHUR C. "Discussion on Rate Regulation Revisited," *Insurance and Government*. (University of Wisconsin Insurance Series, Vol. II, No. 4), Madison: Fund for Insurance Education and Research, University of Wisconsin, 1960, pp. 128–137.

MICHELBACHER, GUSTAV F. "Competition in the Multiple-Line Insurance Business," *Insurance Counsel Journal*, XXVII, No. 1, January 1960, pp. 138–142.

MORRILL, THOMAS C. "Marketing Revolution," *Best's Insurance News*, November 1956, pp. 18 ff.

MOSER, HENRY S. "Competition and Insurance: Yesterday—Today—Tomorrow," *Insurance Law Journal*, No. 384, May 1955, pp. 305–310.

————. "Operation of Independents Under the Rate Regulatory Pattern," *Law and Contemporary Problems*, XV, No. 4, Autumn 1950, pp. 523–539.

MOWBRAY, ALBERT H. "Competition and Regulation of Rates for Casualty Insurance," *Proceedings of the Casualty Actuarial Society*, VIII, No. 17, 1921, pp. 5–12.

MURPHY, RAY. "Public Law 15 and State Regulation," *Proceedings of the Section of Insurance Law*, American Bar Association, September 1947, pp. 9–22.

NAVARRE, JOSEPH A. "Supervision of Insurance," *Insurance Law Journal*, No. 384, May 1955, pp. 299–304.

NICHOLS, ARCHIE. "The Liquidation of Insurance Carriers in the Common-wealth of Pennsylvania," *Journal of Insurance*, Vol. XXVIII, No. 2, June 1961, pp. 45–50.

ORFIELD, LESTER B. "Improving State Regulation of Insurance," *Minnesota Law Review*, XXXII, No. 3, February 1948, pp. 219–261.

OTTO, INGOLF H. B. "Capacity," *The Journal of Insurance*, Vol. 28, No. 1, March 1961, pp. 53–70.

RENNIE, ROBERT A. "One Out of Three," *Best's Insurance News*, October 1959, pp. 81–90.

RIEGEL, ROBERT. "Rate-Making Organizations in Fire Insurance," *Modern Insurance Problems*. Philadelphia: The American Academy of Political and Social Science, 1917, pp. 172–198.

SAWYER, ELMER W. "Can We Audit the Past in Terms of the Future?" *Insurance Law Journal*, No. 316, May 1949, pp. 362–367.

SMITH, BRADFORD, JR. "Current Developments in Insurance Rate Regulation," *Insurance Law Journal*, No. 445 (February 1960), pp. 75–84.

SPOTTKE, A. E. "Automobile Insurance Rates Make a Barometer of Accident Costs," *Insurance Law Journal*, No. 434 (March 1959), pp. 162–170.

STELZER, IRWIN M. "Economic Consequences of a Successful Antitrust Prosecution," *Insurance Law Journal*, No. 373 (February 1954), pp. 86–90.

————. "The Insurance Industry and the Antitrust Laws: A Decade of Experience," *Insurance Law Journal*, No. 386 (March 1955), pp. 137–152.

STONE, BERNARD R. "Rate Regulation *v.* Rate-Making," *Insurance Law Journal*, No. 385 (February 1955), pp. 107–111.

STRYKER, PERRIN. "Auto Insurance: Battered by Its Own Boom," *Fortune*, LXII, No. 4 (October 1960), pp. 142 ff.

TOOKEY, CLARENCE H. "Expense Problems," *Best's Insurance News*, May 1955, pp. 89–95.

TWAITS, ELMER A. "Casualty and Surety Rating Bureaus," *Best's Insurance News*, April 1959, pp. 29 ff.

VORYS, ARTHUR I. "Insurance Supervision and Current Trends," *Insurance Counsel Journal*, XXVI, No. 1 (January 1959), pp. 43–48.

————. "The Responsibilities of the Insurance Commissioner," *Papers and Proceedings*. Indianapolis: National Association of Mutual Insurance Companies, October 1957, pp. 71–78.

WALLACE, DONALD H. "Industrial Markets and Public Policy," *Public Policy*. Edited by C. J. Friedrich and Edward S. Mason. Cambridge: Harvard University Press, 1940.

"Where's the Cheer in Choas?", *Journal of American Insurance*, XXXIV, No. 1 (January 1961), pp. 8–11.

Unpublished Material

CRANE, FREDERICK G. "Price Policy and Price Competition in Automobile Insurance." Unpublished Master's thesis, The Ohio State University, 1957.

HENSLEY, ROY J. "An Evaluation of Economic Performance of the Property Insurance Industry." Unpublished Ph.D. dissertation, University of California (Berkeley), 1955.

McHUGH, DONALD P. "Federal Investigation of Insurance." Address at Arizona Insurance Day, University of Arizona, February 27, 1960. (Mimeographed.)

————. "The Challenge to State Regulation of Insurance." Address before South Carolina Insurance Forum, February 1, 1961. (Mimeographed.)

National Association of Insurance Commissioners. *Report of Subcommittee to Review Fire and Casualty Rating Laws and Regulations.* 1960. (Mimeographed.)

OTTO, INGOLF H. B. "Regulation of Insurance in the United States by the Federal Government." Unpublished Ph.D. dissertation, George Washington University, 1959.

ROKES, WILLIS P. "Automobile Physical Damage Affiliates of Sales Finance Companies." Unpublished Ph.D. dissertation, The Ohio State University, 1959.